# MENTALLY STRONG
## PARENTS AND CHILDREN

*Raising a Mentally Strong Kids Requires Parent to Avoid the Common Yet Unhealthy Parenting Practice That Rob Kids of Mental Strength*

ALICE HEATHFIELD

# Copyright © 2020

# TABLE OF CONTENTS

# INTRODUCTION

## Understanding Mindful Parenting

M indfulness is the ability to be present at the moment while it is happening. It's about realizing and accepting what's going on and not letting your mind try to change it. Mindfulness has become something of a buzzword lately, but that doesn't necessarily make it any less important. Mindful Parenting is the process of being present, at the moment, with your children. Your care can be the best gift you can give your children, and mindful Parenting is a way to help them do it. Children, especially young children, live quite naturally at the moment. They have very little thought for the past, and generally none for the future. They are fully aware, although not necessarily aware of this. The sensations are immediate: pain, discomfort, happiness, hunger. But as parents, we got away from that world. We are often guilty of focusing on the future, both in the short and long term. We plan what we will cook, buy, eat, dress, and do when we have to leave the house when we return. We tell ourselves that we have to do this to manage, which may be true. At the same time, however, it means that our focus is not on our children at the moment. It can be very difficult to stop and pay close attention to your children. There is always something else to do, whether checking emails, making a call, putting dinner in the oven, or feeding the dog. Training your mind and that of your kids is very important for growth and development.

# CHAPTER ONE

## Developing mentally strong kids

I f you want your children to do well, spend twice as much time with them and half the money. Being aware and careful isn't just about seeing what your kids are doing and responding. It is also essentially about empathy and emotional Intelligence. You cannot be emotionally aware of your children if you do not know them more generally. mindfulness and response to emotions, in other words, empathy, is the key to personal relationships and to educating round and happy children.

Mindfulness is about attention and mindfulness. It requires a non-judgmental approach, which in turn leads to acceptance. The idea is that most of our feelings (unhappiness, fear, anger, or shame, for example) are not real, but constructions made by our minds, based on our past experiences. By becoming aware of how you feel, the moment you feel it, you can examine the feeling more closely, and it becomes much more "all in your head" and not "real." Therefore, you can take control of the feeling, instead of controlling yourself. No one says that you manage not to judge completely, or that you are not afraid and try to take control of what is happening. However, the idea is that when you feel you start reacting this way, you should be aware of it and hold back, simply asking yourself, "How do you feel?" Reacting is pointless, and is generally an emotional response guided by your hopes and attachments, for example, to sit quietly and work or eat in peace; The response is careful, and it may take a moment to notice your reaction and why it occurred, to allow you to form an appropriate response. Therefore, the first step towards mindfulness is to be more aware of your reactions and capture them before responding. To accept, you must be able to feel compassion, both for yourself and others.

Compassion is not critical; it is simply able to "feel" someone else. Some people call it kindness. Cultivating compassion will allow you to forgive yourself when you don't reach your parents' ideal, which we all do from time to time. It will also allow you to accept your children for who they are, not for what you would like them to be.

mindfulness does not mean withdrawing from the world and taking time for ourselves and our thoughts. Far from it, in fact. Instead, it's about being present and aware of life. Remember, mindfulness isn't at all; it's just. It is an end in itself. Once you are mindful, you can accept, but mindfulness does not give you that acceptance. We often hear, "You don't want your life to go" and "Enjoy this, it will disappear soon." Mindfulness helps you accomplish both, and sincerely enjoy and accept what is happening here, right now.

## How to be a mindful parent

mindfulness is the ability to be fully present with the current experience, moment by moment, as it presents itself, with kind attention, without the mind trying to do otherwise. Most of the time, we are on "autopilot," guided without thinking about mental patterns, worried about a future that never comes and a past that is no longer happening. As a result of this, we do feel stressed, anxious, depressed, and synchronized. Mindfulness meditation practices help restore and strengthen the body/mind connection from within, at the moment, increasing health and well-being, despite the external conditions.

As parents, one of the most precious things we can give our children is the gift of our total presence. This is a deeper intention and invitation for most parents as they make room for the practice of mindfulness in their lives. Mindful Parenting takes the profound truth very seriously that we can only give our children what we have given ourselves first.

As we become more aware of our deepest needs through practice, mindful Parenting also involves decoding and responding to our children's deepest needs, rather than being trapped and reacting unmindfully to superficial behavior. Therefore, cultivating self-compassion / love, healthy self-acceptance, and self-mindfulness are essential components of mindful and effective Parenting. Mindful Parenting implies the "inner work" of returning home as a real human being for all. As parents learn to open and "go home" more and more of their unique integrity, letting go of unrealistic expectations, they become more available for their children, seeing, and loving them more and more as they are. Through formal and informal daily practices, mindful Parenting focuses on managing strong emotions, responsiveness, and stress, on improving mindful communication, on respect for sovereignty, on active recognition and on the transformation of maladaptive mental models, as well as on the cultivation of compassion, kindness, and personal care.

The good news is this: we can train to slow down, pause more, make room for a certain "being" instead of "doing" always. We can take a few minutes every day to practice mindfulness and feed ourselves by resting our attention on something very simple, like the breath and the body. This begins to penetrate the rest of our daily lives, and we discover that we can face every day experiences like walking, cooking, and playing with our children more mindfully. It is not an immediate solution, but if you spend some time and energy exploring it, it can be extremely transformative, helping to make your life more joyous and less than thankless work.

## How to present mindfulness to my child?

The most significant thing is to follow the principle of the oxygen mask: first, wear your mask before helping the child. Young children are naturally attentive; they notice the world around them with great curiosity, fascinated by a leaf or stone they find on the way. Adults are often the ones to rush them, teaching them that life is about getting to the next place. The more we rediscover ourselves as mindful, the more we will be able to appreciate and cultivate our children's innate capacity to be present at all times. To present the idea of mindfulness more directly to children, you can use simple games to tune them into their senses. Instead of devouring a piece of chocolate or fruit, you can try to eat it very slowly, savoring the smell, texture, and taste. Spend a minute or two outside just listening to them, inviting them to pay attention to all the sounds they can hear. Take a mindful walk, noticing interesting or unusual things to look at. When traveling by car or train, look for ways to encourage them to look out the window instead of hanging out on phones and other devices.

## How mindful Parenting Helps

Mindfulness helps us to be more aware of our emotions without letting them provoke instinctive reactions. Little by little, we discover how to notice and feel the bodily sensations associated with our stress, anger, or irritation, without having to implement them screaming at our children. In the silent "laboratory conditions" of our mindful practice, we discover that when irritations and unnecessary impulses arise, we can make ourselves feel without judgment, as a natural part of the human being. But we don't have to decide on them. This training helps us respond more calmly when our children press buttons during the day.

## How does mindful Parenting help our family communicate better?

Often we are so caught up in our thoughts and plans that we don't listen to others. Mindfulness helps us get away from our mental chatter and be more aware of others and their needs. We can practice "mindful listening" simply by being present to the other person and giving them room to speak without imposing our agenda. As a person in a family who mindfully practices mindfulness in this way, you may discover that you are shaping it for others and silently encouraging them to listen with more attention and empathy. You can also gather family rituals that encourage reflection: for example, at dinner, they can share something they liked during the day. This can also be a powerful training for children to notice what's good in their lives, even when things are difficult.

# Principles of conscious Parenting

**Here are five main principles of conscious Parenting:**

## 1. Make room just to be, every day

Our lives are lived only in moments. Conscious Parenting depends on being more present, so establishing a daily mindfulness practice is considered the key. Remain seated for 5-30 minutes every day, at the same time and in the same place, making the breathing of the body known as a natural, physical, and felt experience. When the mind wanders (it will!), Don't make it a problem. Just watch when this happens, let go of that "train" of thought and gently bring mindfulness back to the anchor of the breath in the body again. Being present involves maintaining the mind/body connection in consciousness. Research shows that "the mind wanders," that is, when our mind is trapped in the thoughts of the future or the past, separated from what is happening in the body, our health and well-being are compromised. Therefore, it is important to be, at the moment, how you are. We tend to abandon ourselves all day, through activities, distractions, pressures, and requests, guided without thinking. The best gift we can give to our children is our total presence. We have to start with ourselves first. Being present, modeling this ability for your children, is priceless.

## 2. Manage stress consciously

As parents, we often live empty lives, too programmed, in a constant state of low-grade stress. As a result, we seldom bring our best selves to our interactions with our children. As the mind/body connection is strengthened through the practice of mindfulness, it is possible to actively monitor and notice stress or imbalance in the body/mind, for any reason, as we spend the day. We can switch from a stressful and reactive mode to a sensitive mode using the acronym STOP below. You can use it in the pool lane, prepare children for school, etc.

S-Stop. Whenever you feel stress or imbalance, simply pause your consciousness.

T- Take a breath. Simply bring your mindfulness to the body that breathes, letting the sensations of breathing emerge. Also, watch your mind begin to calm down a bit, bringing more clarity. Breathing mindfulness harmonizes the body's cardiovascular systems while calming the "alarm" centers in the early parts of the brain, restoring full brain function. When we are stressed, we cannot think clearly or accurately see any situation.

O- Observe. Just watch as the breath naturally begins to balance the body's systems. Let him hear it. Also, look around. What's going on now?

p- Proceed. After moving to a more careful mode, take a more skillful, appropriate, and appropriate action.

## 3. Adopt the "good enough" parent model

We often keep ourselves too high, striving to be the "perfect" parent. Conscious Parenting includes the reality and wisdom of the "good enough" parent, recognizing that regardless of our best intentions, imperfection and failure are inevitable. So as parents, the way we navigate these days is an important aspect of conscious Parenting. Our children need us to fail sometimes. Otherwise, they cannot separate from us in development.

Furthermore, if we try to deny this reality, our children are not given an authentic model of what it is to be human, warts, and everything else. When these inevitable moments happen, they become opportunities for compassion, learning, reparation, forgiveness, humor, honesty, and kindness. This must be transmitted on an evolutionary level.

## 4. Honor the sovereignty of your children

All children need is to be seen and known, just as they are, separated from their parents. Therefore, establishing healthy boundaries between ourselves and our children is crucial, allowing for clear insight. Honoring the sovereignty of our children does not mean giving them unbridled freedom or too many options. It is about creating greater mindfulness of our unmet needs, agendas, problems, unfinished business, and contrasting dreams. Otherwise, they are too easily projected onto our children. This indicates the "inner work" of conscious nurturing and our ability to view this as separate in consciousness. We must take responsibility for what is unfinished in us, instead of weighing on our children. Can we really see, appreciate, and love our children as they are, different enough and separate from us? Many conflicts between parents and children result in a lack of clear boundaries and emotional separation from the parents. What they desire and what we desire can often disagree. The idea is to learn to recognize and address all of these needs with more skill, understanding, and grace in consciousness.

## 5. Cultivate kindness and compassion.

Nothing is more humiliating, more stimulating, and more heartbreaking than parents. No need to stop, hide, and "target." Therefore, as self-service, we must learn to cultivate the act of kindness and compassion at the moment, especially for ourselves. Most of the time, our children get the best of us, and we can feel empty and resentful. The practice of mindfulness is often referred to as an ongoing act of "self-love" or "self-control." We often seek love, approval, and care outside of ourselves. But, through practicing mindfulness, we can go home alone, go to our best, attend to our needs in a way that only we can do for ourselves. Parenting can be very difficult, so the intention is not to make matters worse. We learn to let go of unrealistic expectations, love, and accept ourselves more and more as we are, and find more and more integrity. Our children need our unconditional love. But we cannot give what we do not possess. Therefore, we must first start with ourselves and experience more and more kindness, compassion, and self-acceptance. As a result, this begins to flow naturally to our children, more and more.

# Parental Intelligence

Why do children do what they do? What do they have in mind? How can parents know the inner world of their children? Have you ever wondered why your son behaves like him? How many times in a single day, you ask yourself, "Why did you do it?" Even small things can throw you away. Your three-year-old daughter lies in putting her toys in the trash. Did he lie? At three years old? Sometimes it's surprising but still disturbing. For example, your teenage son stumbles strangely on a stool in the kitchen and screams when he gets up from the floor to meet a certain girl at a party, something he usually keeps to himself. Why is he telling you now? Does he want to trust you, or has something happened that isn't ready to tell you yet? Parental Intelligence helps parents become "meaning creators" who understand the importance of their children's behavior. Children's actions are communications. A parent faces the challenge of deciphering the message. This is a life change for a mother or father, a new perspective on the behavior of babies, children, and teenagers. With five enlightening steps, parents can solve problems by learning what their children think, want, want, and feel. Are you faced with disconcerting behavior? How can you decide what to do with a behavior if you don't understand it? Before asking, "What should I do?" ask, "What does this mean?" Parental Intelligence helps parents to struggle with the common and sometimes desperate afflictions of family life. It is time for parents to see the distressing behaviors of infants, children, and adolescents as catalysts for change, transforming them into open exchanges of ideas and feelings. Parents and professionals can find a new empathic approach that will redesign families' lives and guide them through the development of the typical and atypical child.

These are the five steps that take you to your destination: Parental Intelligence.

## 1. Take a step back

The first step in parental Intelligence is called Going Back. This means not reacting quickly at this time. At first, this seems contradictory because parents are often taught to react immediately with powerful consequences that teach important lessons. Discipline is misinterpreted as a punishment rather than realizing the true hallmark of discipline: learning. Taking a step back is like the adage: think before you act. Who can discuss it? Let's say you yell at your three-year-old for lying to him about putting his toys in the dumpster, as you said, and responding by insisting that he sit in the corner for a few minutes. It scares and listens upside down. Punishment leads to fear because his tone of voice is threatening. Don't learn to lie. Just learn to be afraid of being yelled at. Instead, stepping back requires slowing down the process when it comes to misbehavior. Taking a break, thinking about what just happened, is a new response to unwanted behavior like lying. It gives you time to think about whether your child has done it before. The search for patterns in recurring behaviors often leads to surprising revelations. When older children lie, for example, this becomes especially important.

## 2. Self-reflecting

The second step is self-reflective. Consider your reaction to misbehavior as a way to learn more about yourself and your child. Are you angry, disappointed, surprised, confused? Does the behavior remind you of something from your past life that has nothing to do with your child? For example, do you remember endless discussions about not listening to your parents who told you to clean your room? Ghosts from the past begin to resurface, allowing him to relive the way his parents reacted. Perhaps screaming was very common in her home as she grew up, in a way she promised not to repeat, and here, unknowingly, she's responding similarly to a three-year-old girl in her toys.

## 3. Understand your child's mind

The third step is to understand your child's mind. This is a crucial step that changes the game for parents. Children act unwanted when they cannot find enough words. Our challenge is to find out what they think, feel, and feel. In general, they already know what's right and what's wrong, so something is going on.

After seeing that you have retired and are calm, they are often even calmer. If you ask why they are worried and promise not to judge or criticize (and stick to it), you may be surprised by the avalanche of words, tears, and complaints. The hard part is listening without interruption and even asking for more because you want to understand with love and care.

Let's say you ask your child, "Why didn't you put the blocks in the container?" It says, "I was still playing." So voila, put them on right away! Oops! He didn't need to lie. He needed some autonomy, a big step for her at three. It was an opportunity to make your decision on when to do the job. She had her thoughts and desires and was ready to express them, given the opportunity. How sad to think he wanted to make an independent decision and end up in a corner fearing his mother's tone of voice, which was probably why he lied in the first place. This child is lucky because Parental Intelligence has been used since he was very young. As she grows older, when this is done regularly as part of her parental life with her, she can learn from more complicated examples that there is an underlying flow of worries, fears, struggles, or other types of problems that result in other misconduct. However, if you try to understand what's going on in your mind, you have the opportunity to discover the real problems behind the behavior. Bad behavior surprisingly becomes a catalyst for communication! This reinforces their parent-child relationship.

## 4. problems solving

The fourth step, problem-solving, naturally comes after the other levels. After learning the problems, like the four-year-old boy who wants some psychology during his playtime or the teenager who wants to confess his alcoholism. Collaborate with your child, even the youngest, on how to find solutions. Her parenting style is modified by seeing the behavior as a way to understand the mind of her now grateful and trusting child.

We had all those moments when we felt so helpless and doubtful as parents. This lifestyle changes it.

When you unlock your parental Intelligence, you don't need to have absolute answers because Parenting becomes a process with your child who knows you will be on their side no matter what. There's much less rejection from teens because they know you're ready to listen with love and careful understanding. It takes time to establish this focus in everyday life. Still, the gains are immense when you discover that your children apply critical thinking and show empathy only for the daily problems they face in their life and even identify with you when you need to!

# CHAPTER TWO

## The role of parents in child development

Parents play an essential role in developing their children. It is the proper parenting guide that develops the child's character. Parenting is an endless work. It is not something you can escape once it arrives, because children need their parents from time to time to stay on the right track. Here are things you need to know about the role of parents in the development of their children. Parenting and child development go handy. The adage, which says the apple does not fall far from the tree and that the branch grows as the twig grows, can well describe the effects of parenting styles on the growth and development of the child. All development is related and cannot be defined in waterproof categories. So, let's focus on how parents can be actively involved to ensure the child's growing years are worthwhile. The role of parents in the child's development is reactive, responsible, and endless. Adjust a child's responses, actions, thinking, and decision making in the following areas.

## 1. Cognitive development

As children get older, positive parents improve their cognitive, social, and problem-solving skills. Positive Parenting also influences their responses and helps them become better humans. Interaction and stimulation are significant in the early years. It is about recognizing problems, managing all situations well, and compiling the features of discipline, time management, and effective problem solving through simple home routines.

The development of children's cognitive and social skills necessary for success at school can best be supported by a parenting style known as responsive Parenting. Reactivity is an aspect of parenting support described in various theories and research frameworks (e.g., attachment, socio-cultural). It plays an important role in providing a solid foundation for children to develop optimally. Parenting that provides positive affection and high levels of warmth and is responsive in ways that are continuously connected to a young child's signals ("contingent reactivity") are the affective-emotional aspects of a receptive style. These aspects, combined with behaviors that respond cognitively to the child's needs, including providing rich verbal input and maintaining and expanding the child's interests, provide the necessary range of support for multiple aspects of the child's learning. Accepting the child's interests with quick and dependent responses to what the child claims support learning, in part, by facilitating the development of the child's mechanisms for dealing with stress and novelties in their environment.

With repeated positive experiences, trust and a bond develop between the child and the parents, which in turn allows the child to internalize this trust finally and therefore generalize their learning to new experiences. This responsive support promotes the child's continued participation in learning activities with parents. Therefore, these affective-emotional behaviors communicate the interest and acceptance of parents, promoting self-regulation and cooperation, behaviors of critical importance for effective learning. From a socio-cultural point of view, receptive cognitive behaviors (e.g., Maintaining interests versus redirection, Rich verbal voice) are believed to facilitate higher learning levels because they provide structure or scaffolding for the child's immature abilities, such as the development of attentional and cognitive skills. Receptive behaviors in this context promote joint participation and reciprocity in parent-child interaction and help them learn to play a more active and ultimately independent role in the learning process. As a scaffold for parents, and it is also considered the key to facilitating the development of children's self-regulation and executive functions, behaviors that allow the child to take responsibility for his well-being.

## 2. Sociocultural development

The children observe the conjugal interaction and how the topics are solved in the family. Teach them a variety of good values that are integrated and crucial for growth. The child learns to behave with others, playing with a common goal, team spirit, choosing suitable friends, and much more.

## 3. Physical development

Achieving age-related goals is not the only goal. Children learn to be healthy, exercise regularly, play in teams, follow a correct diet, and grow in an educational environment through play and learning. Proper parenting guidance can instill a good diet and exercise regime in children to achieve great physical development. Parents should have it in mind that children lead by example.

## 4. Mental development

Parenting styles help children learn innovative ways, accept, and overcome failures, understand discipline, accept feedback, and the concept of reward and punishment. Adjust your response to stimuli, thus shaping your minds.

## 5. Spiritual development

Understanding religion, prayer, knowing the good of evil, being empathetic, having the correct ethical values, valuing your parents, and strengthening the achievement of goals liberates the free spirit in children. Teaching your children to accept and believe more in the common good can help them achieve a purpose. Try not to settle for any particular religion and let them explore spirituality on their own.

# Parent-child relationship

A parent-child relationship (PCR) feeds the child's physical, emotional, and social development. It is a special bond that every child and parent experiences, enjoys, and nurtures. Like other relationships, a parent-child relationship (PCR) * is influenced by each person's behaviors, feelings, and thought. If both partners involved have positive thoughts and feelings about each other and their behaviors respect each other, the relationship is likely to be healthy, functional, and satisfying. In PCRs, if one of these factors is negative or undesirable, there is a possibility that the relationship is not stable and that the needs of one (or both) individuals are not met. In some cases, parents may not have the skills and tools to meet their children's needs, or they may feel overwhelmed and unable to control their children's behavior. On the other hand, a child may not feel safe or cared for if his father does not respond adequately and consistently to his physical or emotional needs. Both are examples of how unhealthy or unsatisfactory PCR can be. For a PCR to be alive, the child must have a parent or caregiver available, warm, and sensitive, reliable, and able to establish appropriate rules/limits. The child must also feel cared for and safe with his parents. Each of these factors helps a child develop a healthy bond with his parents. Studies have shown that some young children who experience trauma can experience less severe trauma-related symptoms if they have a healthy connection with their primary caregiver; Whereas traumatized children without healthy attachment are more likely to experience long-term adverse effects of trauma. The relationship lays the basis for the child's personality, choices, and general behavior. Studies show that a healthy parent-child relationship leads to positive outcomes for children and the family. Parenting is a full-time job with benefits and challenges that grow as the child grows. Here we take a look at multi-stage PCR:

**Infancy**: construction of heat and security. In the first six months, babies cry, eat, sleep, pee, and poop. And in response, parents stop, feed, burp, change, and wash the baby. These interactions lead to expectations. When the child is hungry, he becomes irritated. When the father feeds him, the child's needs are met, and he is happy. The father is also happy to be able to meet the child's needs. When parents perform their primary role of nurturing, loving, and caring for the child, a well-defined and unique parent-child relationship is created. By their first birthday, children are likely to develop a secure attachment to their parents or primary caregiver.

**Childhood** - entering society

When the child becomes a child, the focus is on modeling the child's behavior by teaching, guiding, and feeding him. Parents subtly facilitate the socialization process for the first two years and prepare them to join a social group or society at large.

## Childhood-developing a parenting style

Different parenting styles arise, with one style becoming prominent when the child reaches preschool age. However, it is not possible to consistently use a particular style in all situations; you have to use a combination of strategies to raise children. And the parent-child relationship can best be described by the current parenting style adopted by the parents.

Research shows that children from:

**Authoritative parents** are confident, happy, and focused.

**Overbearing parents** are unhappy, less trusting, and fearful.

Permissive parents without social skills, are irresponsible, and have little emotional control. Neglectful parents have experienced more behavioral and psychological problems than other young people.

**School-age**: discovering a world beyond home.

When the child begins elementary school, there is a change in his attention from parents to peers, but this does not change the dynamics of the PCR. With the child's growing cognitive and social skills, he goes beyond the home environment. This is the moment when communication becomes bidirectional. The child can tell the father what he wants and express his tastes and dislikes. Your parenting style will decide whether the communication will be two-way or one-way. The parenting styles remain the same as the child's growth, and the style used in the nursery continues to influence even in mid-childhood.

Research findings indicate that in the case of:

**Authoritative parents**, children grow up to be socially competent and have high self-esteem.

**Authoritarian parents**, children have low self-esteem, poor social skills, and are very aggressive.

**Permissive parents**, children become impulsive, aggressive, and irresponsible.

**Adolescence**: giving the child personal space

Adolescence is a turbulent and vulnerable phase, which causes physical and psychological changes in the child. Parents need to recognize and understand their children's needs, support them, and give them the freedom they need without being overly controlled. Raising children with love and acceptance by taking a positive approach, even in difficult times, can be an effective way to guide teenagers.

**Adulthood**: speak on equal terms

Adulthood is the moment when stability begins to settle. Parents and adult children can now interact with each other. Adult children are sometimes divided between their parents and the elderly. The balance between the two can be quite stressful. However, most adults maintain a healthy relationship with their parents. The requirements and priorities of a particular family differ from the others. For example, the bond you share with your child may not be the same as what your friend shares with your child. This means that your type of parent-child relationship is different from that of your neighbor.

Here are some principles to guide you in conscious parenting.

There is no "one size fits all" for parenting. However, the following principles lay the basics for positive parenting:

**Set some parenting goals:** if you want to raise a healthy and disciplined child or have a healthy parent-child relationship, identify your goals, and understand what you need to do to achieve them.

**Bring warmth and structure to your interactions**: treat each interaction as an opportunity to connect with your child. Be a warm and caring parent who encourages interaction. Structure your interaction by setting rules, limits, and consequences and make sure your kids understand them.

**The basic rules are mandatory:** the basic rules tell your children how and how not to behave. But having too many rules is not ideal. Regardless of the rules you have, stick firmly to them to shape the child's overall personality and growth.

**Recognize and empathize with your child:** whether it's a happy or difficult situation, recognize your child's feelings, understand them, and assure them that they can depend on you to solve all their problems.

**Take a conflict resolution approach:** when your child has a problem, try to find a solution instead of punishing him. Punishments demoralize your child and lose faith in you. But when you work together with them to find a solution, they also learn. These principles can guide parents on a macro level. What about daily interactions? How can you develop your bond with your child through daily routines?

# CHAPTER THREE

## Types of a child-parent relationship

The types of relationships may depend on your parenting style. A PCR can be broadly classified as follows.

### 1. Safe relationship:

Children feel safe with their parents/guardians and think they will be treated. A safe relationship is created when parents consistently respond to their children's needs. Children who have a safe relationship with their parents are later more likely to be independent and confident. They have good social interaction and can better regulate their emotions.

### 2. Avoidant relationship:

Children feel insecure because parents do not respond to their needs. They are forced to become independent and to take care of children. Insecure parent and child attachments lead to developmental and adaptive problems and behavioral problems such as biting, pushing, and hitting. Children who experience this relationship are more likely to have poor social skills (e.g., abstinence or aggression) and are usually disobedient and impulsive. However, this doesn't mean that they are doomed to fail in life. Change can certainly occur when the child grows up.

### 3. Ambivalent relationship:

Sometimes the child's needs are met, and others are not. Parents respond, but not consistently. For example, parents may not respond directly to a child who is hungry or crying because it is busy with work. But after a while, they can return. These children grow up to be sticky and are often overly emotional.

### 4. Disorganized relationship:

In this relationship, parents ignore children's needs and teach children not to expect anything from their parents. In such cases, one or both parents are likely to suffer from mental illness. These children do small activities and behave unusually. Some of them tend to speak quickly and make it difficult for others to understand their speech or behavior. Are you related to one of these guys? And can you find out which man is better than the others? To develop a better relationship, you need to follow some basic parenting principles, which we will discuss later.

## Why is it important

The quality of PCR often forms the basis for a child's development, which begins in early childhood. For a child to develop normally, he needs a healthy PCR. Children develop attachments with those who watch and who meet their needs. Therefore, when a child forms a healthy bond with its primary caregiver, it suggests that all of the child's needs are met, creating an environment that feeds the child's emotional, cognitive, social development and physical, Healthy relationships and interpersonal interactions in a person's life help regulate brain chemicals and brain functions that also have a direct impact on a child's development. In PCRs, the father becomes a role model for the child. The child watches as the primary caregiver responds to them and others around them. The child learns to adapt his behavior to his environment; therefore, children often repeat parental behavior, which can be transmitted later in adulthood. Children with healthy CRP learn how to form healthy relationships, behave appropriately, and take care of their physical and mental health. They also learn to ask for help when they need it and develop skills to deal with difficult situations that help build resilience.

## How to maintain a good parent-child relationship

Connecting with your child is the crux of healthy PCR. And when the connection is established, your children will follow the rules on their own One way to strengthen your bond with your children is to learn positive interactions in your daily routine. This is how you can do it:

**Embrace your children every day:** Children feel safe when they have the comforting physical touch of their parents. The first interpersonal contact experience was associated with the child's self-esteem, life satisfaction, and social competence in the following years. It has a positive effect on the child's physical and psychological development. Hug your children when they wake up from sleep in the morning and before bed at night and as often as possible during the day. Rub your shoulders, maintain eye contact, and touch your back to show that you care. Older children may not appreciate physical contact or feel embarrassed when hugged in front of their peers. Don't force them. Be subtle and make him understand that hugging to show affection and how you love them is not a bad thing.

**Playing with them:** become a child when you play with your children. This allows them to work with you. Have fun with activities like building Lego sets or pretending with the little ones, or playing video games together, or playing basketball/cricket.

**Laughing together:** Parents don't always have to be serious. Sharing a few lighter moments helps build great memories by keeping your fears in check.

**One-on-one interaction:** Take some time out of your daily schedule to communicate with them about their needs and plan to meet them. Take time for parents and children each day to express your love for them, play with them, and do something together.

**Live in the moment:** How often do you live your moments from the moment your children wake up until you put them to bed? Don't rush your daily schedule like it's something to do. Be present, have fun, and live in the moment. Nothing can be more satisfying than that.

**Brush their hair:** Yes, small gestures like brushing your child's hair will help him maintain the bond. Most of the time, teens or youngsters don't like it when you try, but when you can do it with younger kids. They may not be irritated and may even like it.

**Keep your devices:** When communicating with your children, make sure that their mobile phone is turned off or in silent mode, that the TV is turned off, and that other devices are not visible. These little acts show that you value them more than others and can help strengthen the bond.

**Talk and hug before bed:** Bedtime should be comfortable and not forced. It should be A moment where your children are likely to open up to their fears and concerns. Listen to them and understand their feelings to make sure they are there to solve their problems.

When you introduce these activities into your daily routine, you are certainly laying the foundation for a healthy relationship. Once a solid foundation has been established, you can work to strengthen the bond.

# Advantages of a good parent-child relationship

Here are some positive results from healthy PCR. Young children who grow up with a healthy and safe bond with their parents have a greater chance of building happy and satisfying relationships with others in their lives.

A child who has a healthy relationship with parents learns to regulate emotions under stress and in difficult situations.

Promotes the mental, linguistic, and emotional development of the child.

Help the child show optimistic and safe social behavior.

The healthy participation and intervention of parents in the child's daily life lay the foundation for better social and academic skills.

Safe attachment leads to healthy social, emotional, cognitive, and motivational development.

Children also develop strong problem-solving skills if they have a positive relationship with their parents.

The relationship between parents and children must be not only strong but also flexible because you cannot behave with a ten-year-old boy as you behave with a three-year-old boy. To have healthy PCR, parents need to be responsive, reliable, and loving. Here are some tips to strengthen the relationship:

**Start from the beginning:** mothers attach themselves to the baby from the womb, while the father-son bond begins when the baby is born. Studies suggest that parents who were involved with the child initially had a stronger connection in life.

**Invest time and effort:** the more effort and time you invest in the relationship, the stronger your bond will be. Parents are naturally programmed to love their children, but quality time and effort are essential to demonstrate that love. Teenagers need privacy, while younger children need parental intervention and interaction.

**Prioritize your relationship with the child:** your children are your priority. Show him in action: spend as much time as possible with your child instead of "adapting" him to their schedule.

**Be available:** respond to your child's physical and emotional needs. It is essential to be attentive, loving, and seeing things from the child's perspective.

**Empathic**: Help your children express their emotions. Be empathetic and compassionate and let them express their emotions. This may not be easy if you are a new parent, but a little practice helps. By looking at things from your child's perspective, you can understand the reasons for his bad mood.

**Communication**: Communication with the child must be honest, firm, and friendly. Be clear in stating your expectations, what they can expect from you, and the basic rules and consequences for non-compliance. With that said, don't let the baby press your buttons. As a parent, you have to deal with it maturely and calmly.

**Get involved in their activities, friends, and studies**: parents involved in their children's lives have strong parent-child relationships. Find out what happens to them, understand their academics, and meet their friends. Stay in regular contact with your child's teachers or volunteer at school if you have free time.

**Listen actively:** listen passively while doing your homework and occasionally respond with "hmm" or "OK" between shows that don't interest you. When your child talks with you, quit what you are doing and listen to him. Give them all your attention, ask questions, or repeat what they said. Remember to keep eye contact while talking to them.

**Make family time important:** eat together and talk about your day at dinner. Get used to movies, events, or family outings.

**Trust your child and be reliable:** trust is the foundation of any relationship. Your child should be able to trust you and feel safe. Earn their trust by keeping your promises, giving them privacy, and keeping their trust. However, don't blindly trust your child, but make sure checks are in place.

**Encourage your child:** children need to be constantly encouraged and motivated to develop their trust and self-esteem. If you always criticize or correct them, they will feel that their actions or opinions are not appreciated.

**Respect your child:** treat your kids as individuals and recognize their opinions and beliefs. While you are somehow responsible for forming beliefs and opinions, other strange factors also contribute to this. Respect their opinions so that they respect you.

## Problems that can ruin this relationship

The relationship you have with your children in the early years forms the basis for later years. If the parent-child relationship is affected by various problems, your child's personality will suffer. Here are some common parent-child relationship problems to avoid:

**Physical and mental abuse:** parents (usually alcoholics and drug addicts) can physically abuse the child, while others can verbally abuse them by repeatedly criticizing, yelling at, or posing, which can harm them. Child abuse can turn children into violent adults who mistreat parents and children, creating a vicious circle.

**Lack of respect**: respect is mutual and must be earned. As a parent, you must provide the child with physical, emotional, social, and spiritual benefits. If one of these needs is not met, children begin to disrespect their parents. Such children tend to disobey their parents, break the rules, and trust others more for their needs and wants. Also, you must respect the child in the way he talks and behaves with him.

**Bad communication:** Bad or non-existent communication between parents and children can be frustrating. This generally arises from the parents' belief that their children do not listen to them and that children think that their parents do not understand them. This perspective freezes communication between the two, resulting in anger, bitterness, and pain.

**Codependency**: Some parent-child relationships

are codependent; The child is expected to care for the parents, especially when the parent is disabled or terminally ill. For example, the child takes responsibility for making parents happy, solves family problems, or even takes on daily chores at home. They could also put their parents' needs first and become a codependent personality.

**Mistrust**: When children repeatedly make mistakes or show rebellious behavior, parents find it difficult to trust them. If parents want to restore trust, they must allow their children to demonstrate that they are trustworthy.

## Your child and mental health.

Mental health is the way children feel or think about themselves and the world around them. It depends on how children cope with the challenges and stresses in life.

Children with good mental health:

- feel happy and positive with yourself
- enjoy their life
- learn well
- have healthy relationships with family and friends
- can handle sad, disturbing, or angry feelings
- can recover from difficult times.

Every child desire good mental health to develop socially, emotionally, mentally, and physically healthy. Good mental health during childhood is also the foundation for better mental health and well-being in adulthood. A strong direct relationship with you can positively affect your child's mental health.

Here are some ways to develop your child's mental health and well-being through a loving and supportive relationship:

Tell your child you love him no matter what he does. You can also show him you love him through your body language and non-verbal communication, and also pamper him!.

Praise and encourage your child when he does something good or behaves the way you want.

Find time to talk and listen to your child every day. If your child wants to speak with you, try to stop what you are doing, and pay close attention to him.

Enjoy time with your child. The standard way to do this is to spend time doing things your child likes: reading together, kicking a ball, drawing, playing board games, etc.

Work in positive ways to resolve problems and resolve conflicts between you and your partner, with your child, and other family members.

Encourage your kids to learn to connect with others in the community, for example, by greeting and talking to neighbors, attending local parties, or helping out in a community cleaning. This gives your kids a stronger sense of his place in the world and helps him interact with different people.

# Emotions and good mental health for children

It is normal for children to experience all kinds of feelings: fear, disappointment, sadness, fear, anger, joy, hope, etc. When children can face great feelings or calm down in difficult or emotional situations, they are likely to feel comfortable. Talk to your child about emotions and encourage them to recognize and label their emotions. It can also let you know that all types of feelings are normal. For example, "It looks like you're frustrated that your toy isn't working." I can understand it. '

Model a positive outlook for your child: for example, "Running around the oval seems difficult, but I think I can do it if I take it slowly," or "I'm disappointed that my cake doesn't cook well, but it's OK." I try it again. Support your child if something disturbs her. For example, if your child is having problems with friends at school, you can give him a lot of hugs and assure him that he is there to help him. At the same moment, you can work with the teacher on a plan to deal with the situation.

Help your child manage daily worries so that they don't become difficulties. This can be done by gently encouraging your child to do the things he or she fears without pushing too hard. For example, "Have you thought about trying the choir at school? You sing very well."

Here are some ways to promote your child's mental health and well-being by focusing on behavior:

Provide clear rules of conduct and involve your child in developing rules and consequences. Change the rules and consequences as the child grows older.

Help your child set and work towards realistic goals for his age and ability, such as riding a bicycle without training the wheels.

Help your child learn the attitude to solving problems so that he develops the skills to do it on his own as he grows up. For example, you can help your child solve the problem, brainstorm on possible solutions, and choose a solution to implement.

Encourage your kids to try new things, take age-appropriate risks, and learn from his mistakes. This could include things like trying out a new sport, participating in a drawing competition, talking to your class, climbing new equipment on the playground, etc. Ensure your kids have a healthy balance between the time spent on the screen and other activities useful for their development. This includes socializing with family and friends, being physically active, reading, and being creative.

# CHAPTER FOUR

# Good physical and mental health for children

P hysical health is a big part of being considered in mental health. This is because physical fitness helps the child to stay healthy, to have more energy, to feel safe, to manage stress, and to sleep well.

Offer healthy food and promote healthy eating habits in your family.

Encourage your child to try different physical and sports activities. Trying a lot of activities is good for your condition and energy level. You can also help your daughter feel good about herself as she develops new skills.

Make sure your kid gets what he needs. Quality sleep helps the child manage stress and busy life.

If you are concerned that your child is showing signs of poor mental health, it is best to seek professional help as soon as possible. The doctor can guide you to the services best suited to your family.

Mental health affects the way most people feel, think, and behave. Taking care of our mental health is as important as a healthy body. As a parent, you play an essential role in your child's mental health: You can promote good mental health through the things you say and do and the environment you create at home.

## Helping children build strong and loving relationships

Children and youth must have a strong relationship with family and friends. Spend time together at the dining room table every night. An important person who is constantly present in a child's life plays a crucial role in the development of resilience. This person, often a parent or other family member, is someone your child spends a lot of time with and knows they can turn to when they need help.

Teach your children how to solve problems.

Help children and teens build their confidence, so they feel comfortable:

Show a lot of love and acceptance.

Praise them if they do well. Recognize their efforts and what they get.

Ask questions about their activities and interests.

Help them set realistic goals.

Listen and respect their feelings: It is good for children and young people to feel sad or angry. Encourage them to talk about their feelings.

Maintain communication and conversation by asking questions and listening to your child. Food can be a good time to talk.

Help your child find someone else to talk to if he doesn't like talking to you.

Create a safe and positive home environment:

Consider your child's use of media, both content and screen time. This includes TV, movie, internet, and gaming devices. Consider who can interact on social media and online games.

Be careful when talking about serious family problems, such as finances, marriage problems, or illness, around your children. Children may be concerned about these things.

Allow time for physical activities, games, and family activities.

Be a role model for your mental health: talk about your feelings. Find time for the things you like.

Help children and young people in difficult situations solve problems:

Teach your child how to relax when he is upset. It can be a deep breath, doing something relaxing (such as a quiet activity that you enjoy), taking time alone, or walking.

Talk more about possible solutions or ideas to improve a situation and how you can achieve it. Don't try to take control.

How often do psychological problems occur in children and adolescents?

Mental problems can affect young people of any age. But some situations may present a higher risk for some young people, including:

Unfortunately, too many children and young people

do not receive help early enough. Mental disorders can prevent children and youth from succeeding in school, making friends, or becoming independent of their parents. Children and youth with mental disorders may have difficulty reaching developmental milestones.

The good news is that mental disorders are treatable. There are many different ways to help children and teenagers who have mental or emotional health problems. Getting help early is important. You can prevent the problems from becoming more serious and reduce the effect they have on your baby's development.

What are the signs to know if my child kid a mental problem?

All children and young people are different. If you fear that your child has a problem, watch for changes in how he thinks, feels, or acts. Mental health problems can lead to detrimental physical changes. Ask questions like how your child is doing at home, at school, and with Friends?

## Changes in thought:

- Saying negative things about their self or blaming their self for things beyond their control.
- Difficult to focus.
- Frequent negative thoughts.
- Poor school performance.
- Changes in emotions
- Attitudes or feelings that seem bigger than the situation.
- He seems very unhappy, worried, guilty, anxious, irritable, sad, or angry.
- Feeling helpless, hopeless, alone, or rejected.
- Changes in behavior.
- They often want to be alone.
- You cry easily.
- Show less interest or withdraw from sports, games, or other activities they usually enjoy.
- Exaggerated reactions or sudden outbursts of anger or tears from minor accidents.
- He seems calmer than usual, less energetic.
- Difficulty relaxing or sleeping.

- Many daydreams.
- Use less mature behavior.
- Interaction problems with friends.

## Physical changes

Headache, abdominal pain, neck pain, or general aches and pains.

Lack of energy or feeling exhausted all the time.

Trouble sleeping or eating.

Too many energies or nervous habits like biting your nails, twisting your hair, or sucking your thumb.

**Remember**: just because you found out one or more of these changes doesn't mean your child or young person has a mental health problem.

Where can I ask for help?

There are many ways to help the child achieve good mental health. Sharing your concerns with your doctor is one of them. Talk to your child's doctor: if the behavior described above persists for a while or hinders the functioning of the child.

if you are feeling concerned about your kids mental and emotional health, On your child's behavioral development and emotional health at each visit of a good child. If your son or son talks about suicide or harming you, call your doctor or local mental health crisis line immediately.

## Emotions and mental health

The way we interpret and respond to our feelings has a great influence on our behavior, our choices, and how well we face and enjoy life. Think about all the different feelings you have every day, from surprise to shame, to euphoria and empathy, and how you respond to every emotion. The way you manage your feelings is now very different from when you were fourteen, which is different from your answers at four.

Emotional development is a complex process that begins in childhood and continues into adulthood.

- Emotional development begins in young children:
- Find out what the feelings and emotions are
- understand how and why they happen
- recognize your feelings and those of others
- develop effective ways to manage them.
- As children grow up and are exposed to different situations, their emotional life also becomes more complex. Developing skills to deal with a wide range of emotions is very important for your emotional well-being.

## Stages of emotional development.

Children begin to experience basic emotions such as joy, anger, sadness, and fear. Later, when children begin to develop their self-esteem, they experience more complex emotions, such as shyness, surprise, exaltation, shame, shame, guilt, pride, and empathy. Very young children's emotions consist mainly of physical reactions, such as a heartbeat or butterflies in the abdomen, and behavior. As children get older, they develop the ability to recognize feelings. Your emotions are also increasingly influenced by your thinking. They become more aware of their feelings and can better recognize and understand those of others.

The experience of emotion includes

- Physical reactions, including heart rate, breathing, hormone levels.
- feelings that children recognize and learn to name
- thoughts and judgments associated with feelings
- Signs of action, such as the need to approach, run, or fight.
- Many things influence how children express emotions, both through words and behavior.

These influences include: values and beliefs about appropriate and inappropriate ways of expressing the emotions that children learn from parents and other family members

# How effectively children's emotional needs are met

## Children's temperaments

emotional behaviors that children have learned through observation or experience

The degree to which families and children are exposed to different types of stress.

## Why do children need the help of adults?

Sometimes we all feel overwhelmed. Over time, we will discover what situations or experiences can alter us and how we can control our emotions as they arise. We continue to know what bothers us, and we find new ways to control our emotions throughout life.

Children also have times when they may feel overwhelmed or out of control, but because of their age, they have had less time and opportunities to learn to manage their feelings. When adults respond to children's instructions and help them deal with feelings of insecurity, helplessness, or overwhelming, children feel safe and trust that they have someone to help them when they need it. Gradually, children learn to control their emotions on their own through their experiences with warm, sensitive, and trustworthy adults. When children feel calm and safe, they are more likely to be able to focus and retain their attention, which is critical to their overall development.

## Help children with emotions.

It can help children move from a negative state of unease or sadness to a more positive state, where they feel safe, calm, and ready to interact with their world positively.

Try some of the following tips: Over time, you will discover what works best for your child.

They help slow breathing (blow bubbles or pretend to blow out birthday candles) and encourage them to breathe deeply.

Encourage children to imagine being a rag doll and shaking. This helps to release the tension that can be maintained in your body.

Help children imagine a favorite nap and pretend. This encourages children to close their eyes and relax.

Develop a strategy to use when you feel out of control, such as having a calm thought or image; take your time reading a relaxing story together; or talk to you or another supportive adult about how they feel.

Express your emotions productively: This could include drawing, sourdough, or reciting your feelings with toys.

Increase your hormones to "feel good" through exercise, positive social experiences, a healthy diet, and plenty of rest.

## Parent-child interaction

The parent-child relationship is considered one of the most influential, meaningful, and meaningful relationships in an individual's life. Parent-child communication nurtures their bond and roles to socialize children (e.g., sex, career and work, relationship values and skills, and health behavior), provide social support, show affection, understand their life experiences, conflict, manage private data, and create a communication environment for the family. The way parents and children handle these functions changes over time as their relationship adjusts to the periods of development in their lives. Even moms and dads can respond differently to their children's changing needs, given the unique relational cultures that generally exist in mother-child relationships compared to father-child. Parenting is one of the most beneficial and challenging things you are likely to do in your life. And what makes it even more difficult is that they don't come with instructions! The opportunity for social interactions with parents is important to the growth of all children. Social interactions give children a sense of "themselves" and teach them what parents want them to do. Social interactions for young children generally take place within the family, but as children grow and develop, they want to play with other children.

Therefore, children's interactions with parents must be positive. Parents are their children's first teachers! By interacting with a parent, children learn social skills, such as sharing, working together, and respecting the things of others.

Additionally, young children also learn to communicate and develop fine motor skills. These are some of the ways you can interact positively with children daily... during this time of year, it is important that our children have our "presence" and not just "gifts." Our time and positive contact with our children can be the best gift we can give, and it's cheap! Here are some easy ways to interact positively with the baby every day:

"Capture" your child with positive behavior and congratulate him.

• Limit words like "no" or "no."

• Learn positive behavior instead of telling your child what not to do. • Set limits and expectations

• Learn the behavior you would like to see on your

child's display

• Play with your child as much as his time allows playing is important to the child's development

• Ask open-ended questions and listen to your child making eye contact

• Read to your child every day • Don't be afraid to go to a child's level sometimes going to a chair or the floor can be better for both parents and children.

# Ways to strengthen interaction with children

It is wise to spend time with your children not only when they are young, but also when they are teenagers. The time they spend together helps the family make memories - these are the things your children will remember as they grow up and start their own family. Spending time with children is not just about helping them do their homework or getting them to do their homework; It can be a simple but fun thing to do together.

Here are some ideas for you:

**Read a story together.**

You can do this with young children. It shouldn't be a boring activity where you read, and your child listens. You can make the moment interactive by asking your child what they think next. Or let your child participate by making animal sounds or sound effects in the story. If it's a story both of you are familiar with, they could also act as a theater.

**Sing songs together**

This is a great bonding activity if you're in a car on a long trip, in a traffic jam, or even when you're on vacation out of town. Alternatively, you can also make time to sit in a room with your child, insert the CD, and sing. You can also have fun dancing to the music and songs.

**color together**

This is also for young children. Children sometimes

get bored if you ask them to stay still and just color. Often you will find that after five minutes they try to do something different or they will do what they do. But as soon as you sit down and color, they suddenly seem more interested. Coloring with your child is a great opportunity to chat, ask him about his day, why he likes certain colors, etc. It can even show you how to mix colors and shades. Dyeing can also be therapeutic for adults.

## Play games

Try to spend time with your children. You can try board games or card games. Do this a few times a day. The session or play some different games. Maybe you have Friday night as a game night. While playing, you can also talk to your child about other things and teach him to be competitive without being a bad loser.

## Walk to the park

This is a great activity to keep both of you in shape. They could ride a bike, jog, run, or just play soccer together. Or you can even walk with the dog.

## Bake and cook

Let your child help in the kitchen when cooking or baking for the family. It may start as a chore for him/her, but once they start learning, they will know how to help you without being asked. And this can be a great opportunity to teach them how to cook and bake, too. You will be amazed at what they will remember when they grow up and leave the nest.

## Plant seedlings and do yard work.

As she walks through the garden and the weeds, she teaches her son how to water the plants. So, plant some seedlings and let your child take care of that plant as it grows. It is remarkably a great way to teach your child to love nature by sharing your love of gardening with him.

## Have a covered picnic

It would be nice to have a picnic in the garden, but let's be practical, in Malaysia it is too hot and humid to have a picnic outdoors. So why not have a covered picnic instead? You can even make it special by making it just for you and your child. Grab some tea treats (sandwiches, cakes, sandwiches), and you can even ask your child to "treat" their bears and dolls.

## Host a party for two

This is almost the same as a picnic, except you can have music, dancing, games, and even a gift for your child. If you want to save money and want your child to feel special on his next birthday, this party is for both sides.

## Visit an orphanage and play with other children.

This is something you can do with elementary school children to introduce them to the idea of charity and caring for the less fortunate. Hopefully, they will leave an impression, and they will learn to appreciate what they have at home.

## Disguised games

This could be more for elementary school kids. If you have a lot of shoes, scarves, hats, or costumes, it's fun to play in costume. Your children will love it, and it will help them develop their imagination and creativity.

## Arts and crafts

This is something you can do easily and really shouldn't cost more. Look around the house to see what you have: wastepaper, glue, scissors, paint, and egg cartons. Use your creativity and create what you have at home. Crafts are not about buying kits that cost RM39.90 and producing stained glass or a picture frame. You can use things you no longer want and do something creative with them.

## Have an impromptu session with toy instruments.

This is more for toddlers and kindergartens. Drop and jam with your son/daughter. It doesn't have to follow a tune or be musical. It can be an opportunity to play music with your children. They would love to see you play one of their toy instruments. Don't forget to relax and enjoy the "play" instead of the "music" part. If you are musically inclined, you can introduce the concept of rhythm to your child.

## Take a walk in the garden to find interesting things.

They can be strange or unusual looking stones, or cute leaves and sweet snails. You can even play m, e Spy. This is just a way to do something together in the garden and away from television and video games.

## Photographic project

Take lots of photos together in funny poses and funny faces. Print them out and place them in a large photo frame. This could be a Christmas gift or a birthday gift project for someone else in the family, maybe grandma or grandpa.

## Stone painting

This is an extension of arts and crafts and garden walks. Pick a brick from the garden, take out the paint and brushes, and start painting.

## To paint the nails

This is for the girls. They will love it. You can play beauty salon. Try different colors and see how you like them both.

## Make clothes for dolls.

Another activity you can do with your young daughters. Keep it simple and involve your daughter in fabric selection and easy design decisions. However, you should sew as simple as possible.

## Wash the car

Teach your children to help wash the car. At first, they may complain that it is hard work, but if you make it fun and even competitive, they will want to do it again. Plus, it's a great opportunity to play with soap and water!

## Have a tea

Your children love to go out with you for tea. Find a chic and elegant place for English tea and muffins or scones. Dress them up for the occasion if you want it to be special. However, girls can enjoy this more than boys.

# CHAPTER FIVE

# Child development

A child's development refers to the sequence of physical, linguistic, thought, and emotional changes that occur in a child from birth to early adulthood. During this process, a child becomes dependent on his parents/guardians for greater independence. The development of children is strongly influenced by genetic factors (genes transferred from their parents) and events in prenatal life. It is also influenced by environmental facts and the child's learning ability. The development of the child can be actively promoted through targeted therapeutic interventions and "good" practices at home, recommended by occupational therapists and speech therapists. Psychological and emotional changes that occur in people between birth and late adolescence. Throughout development, the person evolves from addiction to growing autonomy. It is an ongoing process with a predictable sequence but has a unique course for each child. It does not proceed at the same pace, and each step is influenced by past development experiences. Since genetic factors and events during prenatal life can have a significant impact on developmental changes. Genetics and prenatal development are generally part of the child development study. Related terms include developmental psychology, which refers to lifelong development and pediatrics, the medical branch associated with childcare.

Developmental changes can occur as a result of genetically controlled processes known as

Maturation or due to environmental and learning factors, but generally an interaction between the two. It can also occur due to human nature and the human ability to learn from the environment. There are several definitions of periods in a child's development since each period is a continuum of individual differences from start to finish. Some age-related development periods and examples of defined intervals are:

- newborn (age 0-4 weeks).
- infant (age four weeks - 1 year).
- baby (12 months to 24 months).
- kindergarten (2 to 5 years).
- schoolchildren (from 6 to 12 years).
- Teenagers (13-19 years).

Promoting children's development through parent education, among other things, promotes excellent children's development. Parents play q a crucial role in a child's activities, socialization, and development. Having multiple parents can stabilize a child's life and thus promote healthy development. Another influential factor in children's development is the quality of their care. Childcare programs can be useful for children's development, such as learning skills and social skills. The optimal development of kids has considered it is important to understand the social, cognitive, emotional, and educational development of children. Greater research and interest in this sector have led to new theories and strategies, with particular attention to practices that promote development within the school system. Some theories attempt to describe several conditions that shape children's development.

## The importance of the child's development

Observing and monitoring children's development is an important tool to ensure that children respect their "developmental milestones." Developmental milestones (a "free" list of developmental skills believed to be mastered at approximately the same time for all children, but far from accurate) serve as a useful guide to ideal development. By monitoring a child's developmental progress at certain age indicators with these random time intervals, a "log" is allowed to make sure the child is roughly "on track" for his age. Otherwise, this developmental milestone check may be useful for the early detection of any developmental disabilities. This monitoring is usually done through services for children/mothers and pediatricians such as infants and young children, and then through assessments of preschool and school literacy. The quickest possible identification (and, if necessary, early intervention) of development challenges can be useful to minimize the impact that these development problems can have on the development of skills and the subsequent self-confidence of a child or serve as an indicator of possible future diagnosis. Development milestones or milestones checklists are used as a guide for what is "normal" for a particular age group and can be used to highlight areas where a child may be left behind. However, it is vital to remember that while children's development has a predictable sequence, all children are unique in their developmental path and, over time, reach many developmental milestones.

## Children's developmental problems

Problems in the child's development may develop due to: genetics, birth states, presence of a specific diagnosis or medical factors, and lack of opportunities or exposure to useful stimuli. A specific assessment of the most appropriate professional (who may initially be a doctor or pediatrician, then an occupational therapist, speech therapist, psychologist, and physical therapist) can provide clarity on developmental problems, and level of care, as well as help, formulate a plan for overcome challenges. Since the child's development process involves the simultaneous development of multiple skills, it may be advantageous to consult several professionals. Overcoming developmental challenges is crucial to maximizing friendship and developmental speed, minimizing the gap between a child's ability and their older peers, the child's trust, and the parents' frustration. By the child and assistants.

## Milestone in child development

Developmental milestones are physical behaviors or abilities that are observed in infants and toddlers as they grow and develop. Moving, crawling, walking, and talking are considered milestones. Milestones vary by age group. There is a normal interval in which a child can reach each milestone. In some children, walking can be, for example. Start as early as eight months. Others run for up to 18 months and are still considered normal. One of the reasons why the first years of the child's visit to the caregiver are to monitor the child's development. Most parents also see some milestones. Talk to your child's provider if you are unsure of your child's development. If you look closely at a "checklist" or a schedule of developmental milestones, parents can be upset if their child doesn't develop normally. At the same time, signs can help identify a child who needs more detailed monitoring. Research has shown that faster development services start, the better the outcome. Examples of developmental services are speech therapy, physical therapy, and developmental care.

Here is a list of somethings you can see children of different ages doing. These are NOT precise guidelines. There are many different rhythms and normal development patterns.

## Newborn - birth to 1 year

Able to drink from a cup

Able to sit alone without support

babbles

Show social smile

He gets the first tooth.

Playing peek-a-boo

Place the cart vertically.

Roll yourself

Says mom and dad with the correct terms

Contains "NO" and stops activity in response

Go while holding onto furniture or other supports.

## Children: 1 to 3 years.

Able to eat independently with minimal waste

Able to draw a line (if shown)

Able to run, turn and walk backward

could say the full name.

Able to go up and downstairs

Start pedaling the bike.

You can name images of common objects and indicate body parts.

With a little help, she dresses.

Imitate someone else's speech, "repeat" the word

Learn to share toys (without adult guidance)

Learn again (if indicated) while playing with other children

Can correctly recognizes and feels the colors.

Recognize the differences between men and women.

Use more words and add simple commands.

Use the spoon to feed yourself.

## Children from 3 to 6 years old.

Able to draw a circle and a square

Can draw stick figures with two or three functions for human

Let's jump

Balance better; you can cycle.

Start by recognizing written words, start literacy.

Catch a bouncing ball

He likes to do most things independently without help.

He likes to rhyme and word games.

Jump on one foot

Ride the trike well

School starts

Understand the dimensions

Understand the concepts of time

## School-age - 6 to 12 year

Start gaining skills for team sports like soccer, T-ball, or other team sports.

Start losing "baby teeth" and get permanent teeth.

Girls begin to show armpits and pubic hair growth, breast development.

Menarche (first menstruation) can occur in girls.

Bulb recognition becomes important.

Reading skills are further developed.

Important routines for the day's activities.

He understands and can follow various instructions below.

## Adolescent - 12-18 years

Height, weight, sexual maturity in adults.

Children show growth of armpits, chest, and pubic

hair; Voice change; and enlarged testicles/penis.

Girls show growth of armpits and pubic hair; breast development; Menstruation begins.

Peer acceptance and recognition is essential.

## If the child is left behind

Don't panic if your child doesn't match the timeline. "Most of the time there are little problems" "Often there is not even a delay. Sometimes a parent does not offer opportunities to the child. For example, a child cannot sit alone because it always takes place instead of having time on the floor".

Another common explanation is premature labor. "Premature babies may not have the same speed and muscle development," and this can cause a slowdown in motor skills that generally goes away over time.

When children speak or understand slowly, the likely culprit is hearing loss from recurrent ear infections. A less common cause is autism, especially if the child also has difficulty interacting with people socially. Children who are exposed to many languages may also experience delays in expressive language but generally reach two years.

Other causes of significant delays include genetic conditions such as Down syndrome and developmental disorders, such as cerebral palsy or intellectual disability. In some cases, the cause of the delay is unknown.

**Early intervention is the key.**

Some children have severe developmental disabilities, and many others have moderate delays in language and motor skills. However, less than half of children with developmental delays are identified before school starts. Studies now show that children who are taken early do better than children who are not. " Physiotherapy for significant motor delays

Occupational therapy for fine motor delays

Evaluation of hearing and speech therapy for language deficits

Special preschool classes for children with autism spectrum disorders and other delays.

"Early intervention not only improves the functioning of the child but also improves the parent-child relationship and the understanding of the condition by the parent." "In general, when an intervention is introduced, there are long-term benefits for the child and the community, such as better school performance and less contact with the young legal system."

Language deficiencies are of particular importance for a child's professional potential. "If children have significant language deficits at the age of 2, there is a possibility of learning difficulties at a later time", so how early should they act? "Even after 12 months, if you have a baby who is very calm, doesn't chat or doesn't answer your voice, you should get an evaluation."

## How parents can help

Here are some tips to stimulate your child's development:

- Place the babies on the stomach while you are awake to develop the neck and back muscles. Create a safe home environment and place the children on the floor to find out
- Give older children some time out where they can run and jump
- Give the toys different structures that encourage children to explore with their fingers. Provide age-appropriate puzzles, blocks, paper, and crayons.
- Encourage older children to eat.
- linguistic competence
- Play music for babies to stimulate hearing.
- Talk with your child
- Read for your child
- Name the objects by indicating the images in a book.
- Social interaction
- Laugh with your baby
- Limit TV and play with your child

# CHAPTER SIX

# Understanding children's development, why it matters

C hild development is a process that all children go through. This process includes learning skills and mastery, such as sitting, walking, talking, jumping, and tying shoes. Most children learn these skills, called developmental milestones, during predictable periods. Milestones are developed later. This means that a child must develop certain skills before he can develop other skills. For example, children will learn to crawl first and get up before they can walk. The goal of each child is based on the latest goal developed.

There are five main development areas where children develop skills:

**Cognitive development:** this is the ability of the child to learn, perceive, and solve problems.

**Social and emotional development:** this is the

ability of the child to interact with others, including self-sufficiency and self-control.

**Development of language:** this is the child's ability to understand and use language.

**Development of motor skills**: this is the child's ability to use small muscles, in particular hands and fingers, to lift small objects, hold a spoon, turn the pages of a book, or draw a colored pencil. Use to draw.

**Develop increasing motor skills -** This is the child's ability to use large muscles. Through extensive research, we now know that neurons can continue to make connections with adulthood. However, the fact is that the brain grows very fast with billions of neurological connections made during the first three years of life, so children must get adequate exposure to the five areas mentioned above from the beginning.

Although the digital age has expanded the skills and knowledge of young children, it should never replace their exposure to achievements. Every child is an individual and can reach the developmental stages sooner or later than his peers. However, there are certainly times when most children reach a milestone. And developmental milestones do not end when children are six or seven years old. All five areas continue to develop until the age of 21 for most children, especially children. Although gross motor development, motor skills, and speech and language have reached a plateau, cognitive and social development will continue to increase. Going to a classroom that is completely unprepared for those we teach will make progress very difficult and cause great frustration for students and us. Our expectations should be high, but not higher than what the child can give us during development. It is not a goal in itself, but rather a springboard that teachers can use to evaluate and work. We must also put in mind that children are individuals and will not develop at the same rate in all five areas.

# Why is the development of young children important?

You can, however, guess why children need to develop and grow. They can't be kids forever, no matter how intelligent they are. But professionals who work with kids are much better sound in helping them learn if they understand how to grow. "By paying attention to development, teachers can understand what kind of environments children need." By promoting the right environment, children can develop their confidence and explain some of their behaviors, explains Snipes. "By understanding early childhood development, teachers can manage their class more effectively, but most importantly, it helps children develop a strong sense of trust and determination." Having a solid foundation for what's going on in these little minds will give you a much better idea of what they need to thrive. It is also advantageous to detect development problems early.

"Children education professionals should know how to use screening tools if they suspect there is a delay and how they can help parents seek help.

**Important areas for the** development of young children.

Early childhood development is slightly easier to understand if you break it down into learning categories. The CDC distinguishes early learning into four main areas:

- Social and emotional
- Language / communication
- Movement / physical development
- Cognitive (learning, thinking, solving problems)

In healthy children, these areas are important for growth and development. When considering a learning environment, these growth areas intersect, for example. Social and emotional awareness has often increased during the kindergarten years by language and communication. Or young children can solve problems and make cognitive discoveries through movement and physical growth. But if you understand development as a whole, you see that children's education goes far beyond letters and numbers. "We often focus on creating a linguistic environment using colors, numbers, and shapes, but we ignore the emotional vocabulary of the child," says Yates. Omitting an important element, such as emotional expression, can make learning difficult for young students.

# The Four Important Aspects of Child Development

The development of the child is strongly influenced by genetic factors (genes have passed from their parents) and events during prenatal life. Environmental facts and child learning skills also influence the child's development. The development of the child can actively improve through a specific therapeutic intervention and the practice of the "right" house, recommended by professional therapists.

# Why is child development significant?

The observation and monitoring of child development are a vital tool to ensure that children are with their "miles milestones." Millaves de Development (a "loose" of development skills that are believed to be mastered simultaneously for all children, but that are far from the extension) act as a useful development guide. When the progress of the development of a child occurs, in particular, age indicators against these arbitrary time frameworks allow a "registration" to ensure that the child is approximately "on the track" for his age. Otherwise, this control of milestones of development can be useful in the first detection of any progress. This 'check' is usually carried out through services for children/mothers and pediatricians, such as babies and children, and then through assessments of skills to kindergarten and school. The first possible detection (and the treatment of the early intervention, if applicable) e development challenges can be used developing minimize the impact that these development sobs can have in the development of a child's ability and, subsequently, trust or acting as possible.

The listings or graphics of control of marketing milestones are used as a guide on what is "normal" for a particular age group and can be used to highlight all areas where a child could be delayed. However, it is essential to understand that, although the development of the child has a predictable sequence, all children are unique in their development trip and, sometimes, comply with the numerous development milestones.

The development of the child implies the biological, psychological, and emotional changes that occur in humans between birth and adolescent conclusion. During the event, the only human progress of addiction to autonomy. It is a continuous process with a predictable sequence, but it has a unique course for each child. It is not progressed at the same rate, and each phase is influenced by previous development experiences. Since the factors and genetic events during prenatal life can strongly influence changes in development, genetics, and fetal development, usually a part of the study of child development. The related terms include the psychology of development, referring to the progress throughout life, and pediatrics, the branch of medicine related to childcare.

## The four critical aspects of child development:

The search shows if your child regularly plays games with packages based on violence and aggressiveness, he is at risk of significant aggressive behavior. Furthermore, some games promote gender bias and irresponsible sexual behavior. Excessive video games are becoming instead, in today's society. Have you ever heard about this? "Don't you just play your children? They give you some damage"? And this is true because, why wouldn't they do it if they spend so many hours in front of the computer that practiced the game's ability to become an "addict"? Yes, each of us is a player to some extent. However, when it comes to choosing from some aspects of the development of children and video games, I believe that loving and loving parents would dare to doubt here. Therefore, we discuss four critical elements of children's development; all parents must emphasize.

## Visible Development

Many of us can cover this story; Oh, I'm tired after work, and I do not have the energy to go out and kick a little football or play with elastic games with my son. Let's put it like this. If you find out that this was your final day on earth, will you pass today with your child to play fun training games? Know the answer, right? The emphasis here is not to make you reason that this is your final day, but to connect the brain about how important it is to commit to the physical development of your children. Your healthier child is growing now happier than you will be later, right? So, he invests in his son taking immediate actions. Use your imagination, come out and play aloud with your child today, tomorrow or past this weekend and light up, but regularly.

## Social Development

Instead of sitting in front of the computer and playing a shooting game, I suggest you have the privilege of interacting with other children. If you spend quality time in schools or in the Axillaries that interact with others, this should not be a big problem for your child. But if you see that your children are a socially close person, then you have to emphasize this aspect at the expense of the video game. Otherwise, as shown in the survey, the consequences can be harmful.

## Intellectual Development

This is when you need to start a variety of learning activities. It is important not to force your child to intellectual activities, but to build interest. You can stimulate your child's mental growth, paying attention to your interests, consulting a specialist, and obtaining interesting books within that area. You can also buy an interesting e-learning course on the Internet. Keep in mind that the course: it must be fun; Must teach or strengthen some skill (for example, mathematics, language, etc.); It must be competitive (for example, a score must be assigned); And a winner must be appointed and some kind of given award.

## Emotional Development

Allow your child's unlimited hours on your computer to also lead to an escalation of partocratic habits. Very often, children are trapped in the postponement of things when you arrive in a subsequent stage, trying to complete a more and one more round and one more. In this case, and not only, but you also have to be a mentor for your children. Dales instructions. Show the road. Provide incentives and prizes. Teach them what is accepted or otherwise, according to your belief system. But remember to be a goal and always assume the responsibility of what makes your child's value, since it is the basis that you will build your future.

# Things that mentally healthy parent do to train their children

Parents should proactively practice mentally healthy habits to help their children build mental strength. And this should not be complicated; it only spends quality time together, especially doing things like yoga or talking for feelings, which can have a real impact. Parents should give priority to taking care of themselves, model the importance of car care. They should also know the value of the game and fun. They should help the problems that children meet and work through complicated feelings, but they do not fall and adjust things. It is not a coincidence that mentally healthy parents increase strong mental children. And as long as I spend a lot of time talking about avoiding unhealthy habits that derive children from mental strength, it is also essential that parents help children proactively to build their mental muscles.

Healthy mental parents teach, practice, commit and shape mental strength so that their children can learn the skills they need to become spiritual adults.

# Here are ten things that mentally healthy parents do with their children.

1. Pass the quality time with your children: If you are working on a scientific or shopping experiment together, healthy mental parents work to strengthen their ties with their children. They know that the parent-child relationship will affect the future relations of a child, social interactions, and self-esteem.

2. The discourse on feelings: healthy mental parents do not push their children with their emotional disturbance, but they are willing to use the words that feel in their daily conversations. Formation of feelings of sadness, frustration, fear, and anger and encourage children to share how they feel.

3. Practice coping skills: mentally healthy parents do not tell only children to "calm" or "stop crying" without giving them healthy coping skills. They teach their strategies that help them manage their feelings

in a healthy way. Then, they offer high memories like "take some deep breaths" or "Take a break for a minute" to guide children when they need help.

4. The exercise of commitment and strength: not only telling their children to "give hardened." Instead, they work in mental force exercises together so that the whole family can think, feel, and behave in the best possible way. If they are regularly involved in gratitude exercises or practice yoga together, the mental muscle building is a family business.

5. Establish good objectives: the institution of the goals is a precious ability, and mentally healthy parents know that children can learn from each target they settled. Errors, failures, and success all provide valuable life classes. So, if they are creating a goal of physical attitude or the creation of an academic goal every month, they help their children.

6. Take care of themselves: the construction of mental force does not concern inflict pain and suffering: it

implies self-care. Therefore, mentally healthy parents make it a priority to take care of their bodies and their minds. They shaped the importance of a proper diet and a lot of sleep and invited their children to exercise and participate in healthy social activities.

7. Process the thought of the event: If you have suffered the death of a pet or your child, it was cut by the team, healthy mental parents develop stressful events with their children. They validate the feelings of their children and talk about how to deal with the inevitable difficulties of life.

8. Examine the rules: They do not expect their children to automatically understand that there are different expectations of their behavior in the playground with respect to the library. Then, examine the rules and explain the reasons for those rules in advance. This helps children understand what you expect from them and gives them the opportunity to practice their skills.

9. Problems solve resolve: While it can be tempting to rotate and correct issues, healthy mental parents resist what urges. Instead, problems are fixed together with their children. Invite children to share how they could solve their problems and their brainstorming solutions together.

10. Play and have fun: healthy mental parents do not work without joy. They recognize the importance of the game for children and adults. If they are playing ball on the patio or building a castle of the block, relax and enjoy the little moments of life together. Mental force Training continuous activity: Children were not mentally healthy but can learn and practice exercises that will build mental strength. So, the spiritual power trains a continuous priority in your family. Over time, you will help your children develop the mentality they need to achieve their highest potential. And he will also have to refine his abilities on the road.

# CHAPTER SEVEN

## Parents and mentally tough kids

The world that we live in today requires good people. Therefore, parents may go through a lot of pressure that increases their children to contribute to society and the world. Raise children to be healthy mental children who are equipped to face the challenges in the real world, which requires parents, even parents who are also healthy and emotionally. In this way, you will have to see your children fight, pushing us to face their fears and keep them responsible for their mistakes. This makes a hard father! But it is the kind of experience that children need to achieve their maximum potential. Amy Morin, a psychotherapist, and professor at the Norton University of Boston, Massachusetts, gives some suggestions about what parents can do to raise their children to be the best people who can be.

1. Avoid the victim's mentality: if your child has been cut out of his sports team or did not take in ace, that

math test, emotionally stable parents encourage their children to convert their struggles into force, instead of exaggerating their misfortune, trying to help their child identify ways to adopt positive measures despite their circumstances. Refusal and failure are part of life.

2. Do not allow your life to transform your child: children who think they are the center of the universe can grow to be absorbed and entitled. Keen mental parents teach their children to focus on what they have to offer to the world, and not what they are due.

3. Be a guide, not a protector: your kid is the most vital person in his life; it is natural that he wants to protect him instinctively. But keeping children too safe acrobatics to their development. Try to drive your child instead. Allow him to go out into the world and experience life, even when he is afraid to let them go.

4. Do not give your child too much power: if your child is the person who decides what the family is doing this

weekend or eating for dinner, it has too much power. If your child is becoming more as if it were the same, it is not healthy for him/her. Keen mental parents improve children to make appropriate decisions while maintaining a clear hierarchy.

5. Do not wait for perfection: it's okay to have high expectations but wait for your children to be perfect. It is unhealthy. Instead, you recognize that your child will not be, except at all, instead of pushing him to be better than all others. Help them become the best version of themselves.

6. Children also have responsibilities: their children should help at home and learn the skills they need to become responsible citizens. Teachers take responsibility for their choices and give them adequate duties for age.

7. The errors are part of life: what better way to learn is there to learn from your mistakes? Emotionally healthy parents let their children ruin and allow them

to face the natural consequences of their actions. Although it is difficult for you, as a parent, seeing your child commit a mistake, it's worth a long time.

8. Sign to your children to manage their emotions: teach them their feelings and how they can influence them. Help them recognize and appoint emotion. Help them understand that they have options on how to deal with feelings.

9. Encourages children to face the fears of the forehead: avoiding any fearful, the child can never trust. Help your child take worry one step at a time. Encourage them, we praise their efforts and reward them for being brave. This will help you manage your comfort bubble to the real world.

10. Teaching different life capacities: discipline is a crucial factor in increasing healthy mental children. Not the regulations to make them suffer but discipline them to teach them to do better next time. Use the consequences that teach specific skills, such as

problem-solving skills, pulse control, and self-discipline. These abilities will help the child learn to behave in a productive way, even in the face of temptation, difficult circumstances, and difficult stopping.

## Goals in parenting

We are going to begin the school year with empty notebooks, fresh and clean pages. The backpacks are crumbs and forbidden drinks. Children wake up early in advance. We try to go to school a little before the morning bell and start the year on the right path. But the slowly family models begin to appear. Children go to sleep the bedtime later; they wake up with a few moments to save. A child leaves his notebook at school and should scalar to find a friend whose fax works. The past nights fighting against the task for hours, studying the remaining tests for the last minutes, the forgotten tasks, the cameras, and social policy, feel like we were returning instead of moving forward. How can we make this year unique from all others? How can we take our expectations and wishes for a positive change and transform them into a reality?

The transition between summer and school can be difficult for children and parents. Any change in life can bring nervousness, concern, and irritability. Children often have difficulty adapting to new situations, unknown teachers, and the most rigid program necessary during the school year. When you feel overwhelmed, our children can express their emotions through the topic, fighting more frequently with brothers, or withdraw yourself. And parents can find it challenging to stay calm and not get lost with rabies when things are not right. Instead of accepting that this is the way it is destined to be our home, we think of achievable goals where we can work. When we create a plan, we can eliminate unnecessarily and strive failures to help our children feel and have more success.

# Here are some parenting goals

1. Keep your eyes open: Sometimes, we observe that something is not right with a child, but we were distracted. We are all swamped; it is true. We have significant pressures and responsibilities by taking too many directions. The child who sees a little "off," not himself, quickly or more silently than usual, is trying to tell us something. But it is easy to get away this information into a back pocket and just realize that something is wrong when a crisis occurs. Therefore, we think and recognize that the signs were there; we were too worried about paying attention. Do not leave problems with your child in Fester and grow. Open your eyes and look if a child seems sad, retired, distant, more badly humor than usual, or angry. Recognizing whether there appears to be more confrontation between this child and the brothers, if friends stop calling or coming, or if the child cannot find his place at school. Because before meeting it, half of the year can pass, and what could have been a small problem has become a "situation" that requires valuable time and investments and causes terrible aggravation.

2. It is developed to work on relationships with teachers: to reach your child's teachers before the child arrives at a zero hour. "Many parents feel that teachers are teachers if you think there is a problem; it is a good idea to set to know the teacher and ask how you can work on the arm. Too many parents call teachers to ask and accuse instead of saying that we would like to solve this problem together. Before going to the director with a complaint, see if he can spread the situation before. If there are some unique concerns at your home, don't wait for the teacher to discover through your child's performance in class or lack of expertise to keep up with schoolwork and deficient qualifications. When a grandfather falls, if there is a health problem, financial stress, the conjugal astronomy, the problems with the brothers, or any other factor that can affect the academic or social success of his son, would be advisable to enlist the teacher of his son as his own.

3. Work on social skills: Help your child succeed this year, preparing it not only academically, but also

socially. School is not merely to get a rectum; it is also about learning to continue with others and know how to develop friendships. A child who is happy at school is a child who can focus on the studio and do it well. He wants to be there and be part of things. One who believes that the school is for academics and not, unfortunately, social life is a big mistake. How can we teach better our social skills from our children? Establish rules and follow with consequences when necessary. Establish routines for meals and cots that establish stability. Develop your child's ability to get, like another than others, and grow more sensitive. Help your child learn how to show frustration, disappointment, and anger without hurting others or withdrawing at an inmate. Establish basic rules: there is no blow, kicks, nibbling, spit, (no hand-free), and without hurting others through our words.

4. Help children are independent: when children feel as if they were gaining skills and became self-sufficient, they grow more confident in their abilities. See your self-esteem take off. Each year, each child

must be proudly bet on a new skill or greater responsibility for age. We can help our kids grow independent and flourish from: Teaching our children to choose their clothes, dress up as they age, bind their shoes, their packaged shoes, make school sandwiches, take lunch the night before, establishing their own Books of books and science projects should not be the task of parents. Ask your child to help the house and get responsibility instead of waiting to be served. Some skills for which children can help keep the laundry, set up and clean the table, assisting serving guests, cook, cook, and keep their room in order.

5. Contact each child: Our children should never be afraid to talk to us. No matter how long the subject lasts, even if they are wrong, they should not fear that we notice or want to close the door. Our love must be unconditional. It is true, there may be consequences or emotions of disappointment, but they should know that we are here for them. After all, are we your parents and if you cannot believe in our love for them, whose love can we find? Work to communicate with

your child this year. I'm not talking just when I have to call it with a problem as failure titles or after receiving a call from your teacher. I am talking about daily interactions where you share a smile, a kind word, a laugh, a story, or a meal together. The main thing is that you have put time and energy, so you know that you have your life. Talk to your child every day, even if it's just for a few minutes. Put your iPhone down, turn off the laptop when your child (or you) goes home, at meals and historical moments, and when you choose the child from school. Look at it and make visual contact while you have a conversation.

Talk to your child in tone and with the words you want you to use with others. Express your love every day, no matter how difficult it is. I know that a few days will bring unbalanced difficulties and that some children seem more challenging than others. But at least we will know about our hearts that we have done everything possible to help our children successfully surf successfully on the path of life. 6. Show your children counting at the end of the day, we all want to know what it matters, including our children. And as parents, we must show them that we love them unconditionally. They don't have to do something to deserve our love. They can behave or misbehave; we still love them, no matter what. Showing your children issues means they know they are special. Have a unique contribution to this world that can do it alone and that no one else can replace them. Let them know what it especially loves, and the difference they do in the lives of other people.

## Raising Emotionally Healthy Children

If we are honest, many of the emotions of our children can be neglected. We could commit ourselves to juggle or other family commitments, and often we only notice the behavior of our children, instead of their feelings. Here, let's talk with the psychologist at the Ariel Bouncy to know how we can be more in tune with our children and their emotions. As parents, we can weigh many aspects of the health of our defrosting, how many parts of fruits and vegetables eat, the number of times of teeth that you have visited. But a child's mental welfare, his ability to function in society, manage his feelings, and face requests that life is launched, is much harder to quantify. Health professionals have seen an increase in the number of young treated for anxiety and depression. Only in 2017, more than three million adolescents in the United States from 12 to 12 and 17 years old had at least one acute depressive episode in the previous year.

Your child's mental health care may seem daunting, but with simple steps, you can create an environment in which you feel more comfortable discussing your emotions from the tender age. Codependence causes a lot of unhappiness. The research shows that codependence is learned in families and is generally transmitted. It prevents the development of healthy and independent individuals. When parents are coded, codependence is transmitted unless they are aware of themselves and consciously strive to respond to their children with healthy ways that contrast their codependent scheme. But since the condition is learned, it can be prevented and unleashed. The problem is that, as addiction, codependency is characterized by denial. It is also possible that you didn't even realize that you are codes, and you are teaching him without knowing your children, despite your best intentions. The most estimated steps you can take are to work to improve your self-esteem and your communication.

Some of the main signs of codependency are: to be overly focused on someone or something, low self-esteem, not assertive communication, deny or devaluation needs, feelings, and desires, inadequate limits.

A need for control: and how to identify, evaluate, and communicate needs and feelings through interactions with their parents. Therefore, what is taught with their children is fundamental for the formation of their identity and, to a large extent, determines how their sense of self and self-esteem has been ensured. Here are the only healthy families that allow children to become independent and functional adults: the free

MENTALLY STRONG PARENTS AND CHILDREN

expression of thoughts, feelings and observations, equality, and equity of shareholders for all robust communications, reasonable rules, nutrition and support, healthy limits.

As parents, here there are seven key things you can do to make sure your children become independent adults:

1. Allow freedom to information. One of the main features of families and healthy organizations, including countries, is the freedom to express thoughts and observations. The secrets and rules not to mention are universal in dysfunctional families. For example, the aforementioned mention of the death of grandmother or daddy drink teaches children to fear and doubt their perceptions and themselves. Children are naturally inquisitive. This is healthy and must be encouraged, not stacked.

2. Show respect for your children. Show respect means that you feel and take them seriously, that communicates who they are and what they think and

feel they are worth and deserve. You don't have to agree with what they say but listen to understanding the showers that respect them and teach them self-esteem. Talk to your children with courtesy. Avoid criticism, which is destructive for self-esteem. Instead, we praise the behavior you want. You can set the limits and explain the negative consequences of the action you wish to you do not like without calling by name or criticism, as: "It makes me come and other anger when he attends the bathroom for half an hour. We are all waiting", instead of, "you're selfish".

3. Accept the feelings of your children. Many customers tell me that they were not allowed to express anger, complain, feel sad, or even excited. They learned to suppress their feelings. This becomes problematic in their adult relations and can lead to depression. With good intentions, parents often say: "Do not feel sad, (or jealous, etc.)" O, "do not raise your voice." Allowing children to express their feelings provides healthy. Emotions should not be rational, nor does it have to "adjust them." Instead, consolidate

their children, and they want to know that you love them, instead of trying to talk to them as they feel. Express feelings do not mean that they should be free to act on them. Tommy may be angry with her sister, but it's not good to hit her.

4. Respect the limits of your children. Respecting the thoughts and feelings of children is a way of respecting borders. Abuse and verbal attacks violate their restrictions, as well as exposure to unwanted sexual touch and intimacy. This also includes tickets about a child's comfort level. In addition, the property, space, and privacy of children should be respected. Read mail or daily or talk to your friends behind your back are out of bounds.

5. Allow cases of decisions, responsibility, and independence of the children's age. The co-covenants have problems making decisions and being interdependent in relationships. Children need support to learn to solve problems and make decisions. Parents tend to be incorrect at one end or

another. Many children should take responsibility for too young adults and never learn to receive or trust none. Some children are controlled or pampered, become employees, and do not learn to make their choices, while others receive unlimited freedom without guidance. The opposite types are often married to each other. They have a marriage where a spouse takes care of the other, and both suffered. Children resist control because they are looking for self-control. Of course, they push for independence, which is not the rebellion and must be encouraged. The appropriate limits for age teach their self-control. When they are ready to try their wings, they need a guide to help them make their own decisions the freedom to do and learn from mistakes.

6. Have reasonable, predictable, human rules and punishment. The coding grows in the houses where there are no rules or rules that are hard and rigid, or inconsistent and arbitrary. Children need a safe, predictable, and fair environment. When the rules and punishments are unpredictable, hard, or

irregular, instead of learning from mistakes, children get angry and anxious and learn to challenge their parents, authorities, and others. The rules must be explicit and consistent, and parents must be united. Instead of the states and essential punishment in emotions at this time, think about what is necessary and what is reasonably executive, which varies as the age of children and are more independent. Explain the rules to older children, allow you to give you sound reasoning to support your decisions. Research has shown that physical punishment can lead to emotional problems in adulthood. The best disciplines are reasonable, human, and refer to the natural consequences of the wrong fact.

7. Feed your children. You can't give them too much love and understanding. This is not rolled. Some parents use gifts or do not set the limits to show love, but this is not a substitute for empathy and affection, which are needed for children to become safe adults and lovers.

8. Be open "from his early years, children are in constant research of knowledge, and they are experiencing emotions of all kinds," says Ariel. "Transparent communication is an infallible tool in developing a child who is strong and solid in his convictions." Be truthful and open with your kid and explains your decisions and requests to them. This should, in turn, encourage them to open up.

9. Show affection, a guaranteed way to worry about being too loving could make our children. But actually, helps you feel safe and, according to Ariel, you can increase self-esteem. "A child devoid of affection can become an unsafe child." So that you are giving your hugs in preschool many hugs or tell your teenager, I love them, not being afraid to show affection.

10. From your time after a long and agitated day to work, you may not want anything but turn off a glass of wine. But it is unlikely that your child learns its emotions if it seems selfless. Try to book the moment

your child receives his undivided attention. Sit and play with them or take the dog to walk together. Ask them about their day and the way they feel, and remember to give them time to respond, a little silence while you put together their thoughts is fine.

## The right attitude for children to develop mental strength

Not all children are born. While some children are born with natural flavor for numbers and problems, others are naturally athletic and outgoing. However, many things have to do with our genes; the brain is an organ in constant development that can understand new things from an early age. The great news is that you can always improve your young intellectual skills. According to a study conducted by the Preschool Project of the University of Harvard, the importance of personal experiences and the way in which they contribute to the mental development of children between 15 and 8 years is monumental. The good or bad experiences were found during these first years to shape their intellect over the next few years. Both parents play a crucial role in the education of a child. Parents choose what kind of exposure their young people should receive, what kind of experiences they should obtain, and the activities they should enjoy. These make a world of difference.

Cognitive ability is different but can always improve their mental skills in their first years. The executive functions, better known as brain functions, involve the necessary capabilities of planning, time management, and memory-oriented details. Working to improve these executive functions, influence their perceived excellence, not only at this stage but will establish the tone for their future successes. Science raw; this is easily feasible. Mental training activities will accelerate your child's intellectual and intellectual skills in a fashion full of fun. Here are some forms of "revenues" and unlocks the mental potential of your child.

## Increase in concentration:

Memory and level of concentration can be improved by dedicating themselves to some simple activities. For young children, you can use your toys to train them to keep your attention. Take the tail toys in the queue and then gradually remove some of them. Ask them what was removed by one. Help them to name the objects present at home and limit on these objects to strengthen their recoverable memories. If you have older children, you can also adapt the activity mentioned above for your level. Keep many different purposes and ask children to name pure memory. Having words or numbers can improve auditory memory.

## Sleep enough:

sleep plays a vital role in boosting brain functions. Some research supports that afternoon sleep for almost an hour can radically increase cognitive learning skills. While resting, the brain does not receive new information, so it works to "save" the information that has been exposed during the day.

Children require 10 to 12 hours of sleep, while teenagers may need 8-10 hours of sleep.

## Teaching self-discipline:

Children should be taught to self-discipline while opening the way for a potentially bright future. Teachers should be aware of what their priorities are and how they should go and feel them. Time management is an art that must be learned as soon as possible. According to popular belief, self-discipline is much more important than IQ alone. Some investigations also exceed this; It shows that the most critical factor in the success of individual students was power or grid.

## Reading together:

make sure you don't just read your children, but I've also read with them. Read with your child will infuse the habit of reading on your son. Reading and discussing the colitis stories will help you awaken the imagination and creativity of your child. Reading will also arouse the curiosity and ability of your child to imagine things according to his perception. This also acts as a useful, necessary exercise for the brain.

Encourage exercise: exercise actually helps increase learning capacity. According to a study, after exercising, the brain collects the words of the fastest vocabulary. The use of the bloodstream up to 30% continually increases to the part of the brain that deals with learning and memory.

## Taking music lessons:

young children who are enrolled in musical experiences represent a relatively high level of brain development compared to those who are not enrolled in music lessons. It is said that music will help improve intellect among young children for about four years. By introducing them to music and providing a creative output can quickly add a child's musical intelligence.

## Meditation:

It is never too soon to start with meditation techniques to calm and calm your mind. He teaches children some deep breathing techniques to help improve memory emotions and control. Ask them to imagine their breath to be like an elevator. Breathing deeply, the elevator increases; During breathing, the elevator goes down.

## Having a door communication policy:

Parents must have an open-door policy when it comes to communicating with their children. If the children are pretty young, encouraging them to talk. Ask questions. Dales, your time and attention when they fight to form prayers to ask you something. This also increases their self-confidence and trust when it is easier to trust their parents.

## Play with your children:

The time of reproduction is the best gift you can give to your children. Take your time from your busy program to enjoy internal and external activities with your children. Going to picnics on the beach or the park will moderate your child's personal experiences. In this way, the child will be able to know their environment and acquire confidence in interacting with the situation. Children should be encouraged to socialize with other children, so they learn to make friends with favor, share, and respect each other.

Active learning: it depends more on the dynamic learning process instead of opting for passive learning activities. Active learning is a method that involves and challenges the ability to think and learn children who use real and imaginary situations of life. Includes spontaneous events, previously planned and intentional activities, seeking and exploring around the house, or in class. Learning is a continuous process. Enjoy your child in learning activities that involve not only the mind but also the body. If you have a small child, after these ten tips, you will improve your mental skills. These will also maintain mental illnesses, which generally influence people in their previous years, to the bay.

# CHAPTER EIGHT

## Parent and child activities for mental development

What favors healthy brain development in children? Discover the fun brain construction activities for newborns, small children, and preschool children. The early years of life are when the brain development of a child is the fastest, and when more than 700 neuronal connections are formed every second. What favors healthy development during these first critical years? Positive interaction is essential among children and adults who care for them. Every time we connect with children, they are not just their eyes that light up, it is also their brain. First positive experiences with adults to strengthen the links that a child accumulates and helps children be excited, committed, and ready for a learning life. This is called a brain-building, which does not require extra money or additional resources. So, how can you aid your children to have productive interactions? This is where the VR room comes.

**Child Brain Development and Building Basics:** The bright horizons have been collaborated with VOOM to give you fun activities to do with your children. VOOM offers over 1,000 businesses and family tips with children from 0 to 5 years that adapt to daily routines. Every action is based on which VROOM calls the five fundamental concepts of brain building. Look, follow, chat, take trips, and stretch. Think of the experience of parenting as an entry liberation responsibility over time, starting from when the child is in preschool. Your child must learn from the tender age that you are your best defender and cheerleader. At the same time, your work is to keep it safe and healthy by creating reasonable limits—mutual respect, understanding, and cooperation guide each interaction.

Look: Even before the newborns can talk, they show what they are interested in. Look in his eyes, or what captures his eye and begins to build with his son.

Follow: The powerful movements are created when

they let the children take the road and continue to respond to their words, sounds, actions, and ideas.

Chat: You may not seem like this, but the sounds and gestures of young children go to communicate with you. Then, he speaks out loud together, even if they still cannot talk and continue talking while their children grow up to get involved to look at everyone who surrounded them.

In turn: Returning and return interactions between you and your child are some of the most important ways to help development. So be sure you do it at your time while you talk, playing, or exploring with your children.

Stretching: Take time to base you for the last time in what your child says or ask questions about the follow-ups that expand the thought and learning of your child. When you extend the conversation with questions like "What do you think?" Or "How do you feel?" You are also stretching the building moments.

Everyday cognitive Development & Building Activities for Children, here are little Vroom activities you can try with your children.

## Development and construction of the child and infantile brain:

Stairs Account: When your child is learning to walk up and down the stairs, take their hands, and count every step they make together. This will help your child be familiar with the numbers and believe that it is a fun game at the same time! Connecting that the numbers are not just words to memorize, your child is starting to learn math.

Food rhymes: During a meal or a snack, create a verse or a rap on what your child is eating: "There is no slice, no data, we eat rice!" O "The name of your child) is not a rookie, eating your biscuit." Your son will appreciate the sound of words, and if he answers, he also rhymes with his words. Listening to the rhymes and conform to your food fun while helping the child to develop communication skills.

Waterworks: Hand washing or bath Tell your child: "This is hot water (point in the tap); This is cold water. Together they make hot water! This is soap. Soap and water make the bubbles clean our hands. Now, we will ride the bubbles.

## Preschooler and preschool-preschool activities Brain development activities:

Fruit data: when you choose fruit for a snack, you play a riddle game. "Does this sweet or acid orange a crispy or soft apple?" Use the words your child cannot understand and ask him to use his own words to tell tastes. When you eat the fruit later, discuss the conjectures. Using new words and asking questions to help build the vocabulary and the reasoning abilities of your child.

Beat & Repeat: Create a rhythm with two trappings and repeat. Can your child copy it? Ask your child to believe heartbeat with two classes. Every time someone is missing, try again. Then do it three beats.

How many beatings can you get? Four? Five? Are you? This fun activity can be done at anytime, anywhere! Because your child copies his models and creates his, they are developing self-control and learning from their mistakes!

Guess who: Ask your child to think about a family member or a friend without saying who. Let us give you suggestions until you guess who the mysterious person is. Then it's your turn to play the same game with him. This game of enigmas helps your child develop critical thinking skills by understanding essential clues.

**Other activities are**

1.identifies the noises Ask your child to identify listening noises: a shot at the door, the dishwasher, a dog barking, a fire truck, etc.

2. Dai to your son your child the opportunity to select between two options as many times as you can: "Would you like the apple or orange. Do you want to

use your red shirt or your yellow?" "Will we read" good night moon "or 'but not the hippopotamus?

3. Practice the alphabet sings the song of the alphabet and read the books that highlight the ABCs count .

4. Count everything! It has how many apples shopping at the grocery store. Count the volume of books on a shelf. Account the number of butterflies on a page in a book.

5. Indicates forms and color points: Talk about styles, colors, and numbers all day. "It's a square napkin, blue." "We only have a banana on the left."

# Child psychology

To learn about your child while they develop: it can be one of the most rewarding parts to be a parent. Find out how your child sees the world, teaching his son new skills and mentors, while they develop great feelings and changes, is all part of being a father, but it's not easy, how the child grows, crossing progressive stages of development, from birth to adulthood. Environmental, genetic, and cultural factors can influence the event of a child and way quickly progress from one phase to another. It is difficult for children to explain what is happening, much less to analyze their feelings. Here's where children's psychology can help you provide essential and valuable information. What is child psychology?

Child psychology is the learning of the subconscious and conscious child development. Child psychologists observe how a child relates with his parents, themselves and with the world, to understand their mental development. How do the children's lives change, and what role do children's psychologists have on children who support them? The psychology of children is a broad area, covering how people change while growing from birth through adolescence and, trying to explain how these crucial changes occur, they are three years, seven years, seven years old and adolescents are different only for their experiences in the world, since the psychology of children is so vast and tries to answer any questions, researchers, and professionals often separate development into specific areas. In general, these tend to map the physical, cognitive (thought, learning, memory, etc.) and social/emotional development. Child psychologists try to make sense of all aspects of child development, even as children learn, think, interact, and respond emotionally to those around them, make friends, include emotions and personalities, temperaments, and skills through.

Children typically reach the "development milestones. These milestones reflect skills, such as walking and speaking, that are obtained from most children at similar times. Among other things, we are focused on trying to tell how children reach these milestones and how one, social and cultural factors may influence how we develop.

Psychologists are also specialized in different areas of interest: while a bit of concentration to support children in school environments (educational psychologists), others focus on the support of children with atypical development (clinical psychologists).

How is it useful? All want your child to have a healthy development, but it is not always clear if the behavior of a child is a symptom of a normal phase in progress or an anomaly. Child psychologists can help you understand the difference. Understanding the normal and abnormal psychological models of a child can help parents understand how to communicate and connect to their child, teach their children's coping mechanisms for emotions management, and help their child progress and prosper in each new development phase.

Son psychologists can also identify animal behavior in advance, helps detect the root of common behavior problems, such as learning problems, hyperactivity or anxiety, and help children work through the trauma of the first They can also help prevent, evaluate and diagnose delays and development abnormalities, such as autism. Children's psychology studies the interaction of some significant development areas.

## Importance of child psychology in understanding your kids

We look at the five of the main areas covered by the study of children's psychology and what teaches us how children's ticks are made. Is the psychology of children doing, the psychology of the child was a bizarre concept? During medieval times, for example, children have been seen as nothing more than small versions of adults. They were treated, and even clothes, as adults. Today we know that childhood is a compelling moment in a person's life. The events that happen when we are young, even small, apparently insignificant, can have a direct influence on how we perceive and behave as adults. The study of the psychological stages of children, and in particular, since these processes differ from those of adults, as they develop from birth to the end of the announcement, son's psychologists work with children and adolescents to diagnose and help solve problems Causing emotional or behavioral issues, as a learning disability, attention deficit disorders, hyperactivity, anxiety, and depression—even children for developmental delays, autistic spectrum disturbance signs, and other problems influencing development.

## Areas of child psychology and what they teach us

1. Development, the study of child growth, is often shared into three broad areas: physical, cognitive, and emotional-social. The physical event, which generally occurs in a relatively stable and predictable sequence, refers to the material changes of the body and includes the acquisition of specific skills, such as coordination

of the gross engine and the engine. Meanwhile, cognitive, or intellectual development refers to the processes that children use to obtain knowledge and include language, thinking, reasoning, and imagination. Since social and emotional development is so correlated, these two areas are often joined together. Learning to connect to others is part of a child's social development, while sensitive building involves feelings and expression of emotions. Confidence, fear, trust, pride, friendship, and humor are part of their emotional, social event. When they can be divided into categories for the most comfortable understanding, the physical, cognitive, and social areas of a child's development are all inextricably, development links in a city can strongly influence another. For example, writing words requires both motor skills as cognitive skills. And, like research has announced the different areas of development, it also shows that development follows the key models or principles. Understanding these principles had a significant influence on how it matters, treating and educating children today.

2. The development of military milestones is an essential way for psychologists to measure a child's progress in various vital development areas. Essentially, they act as control checks in the development of a child to determine which is the average child who can do in a particular era. Knowing the milestones for several ages helps the psychologist understand the healthy development of the child and also helps to identify potential problems with delayed development. For example, a child who has 12 months can usually support and support his weight while keeping something. Some kids at this stage can even walk. If a child gets to18 months of age, but he can still walk, he could indicate a problem that needs further investigation. The psychologists of the company analyze the four main categories of milestones, which follows the main areas of development discussed above. First of all, there are milestones, which belong to the development of gross and refined motor skills. Secondly, there are cognitive or mental milestones, which refer to the attitude to the child's development to think, learn, and solve problems. Thirdly, there are

social and emotional milestones, which belong to the child's ability to express emotions and respond to social interaction. And finally, there are milestones of communication and language, which involve real-verbal and non-verbal communication skills.

3. Behavior children can be wrong, caused, and impulsive from time to time. Misunderstanding between parents and children is also inevitable as the last struggle, of the terrible "two" "through adolescence, to affirm their independence and develop their own identities. These behaviors are a normal part of the growth process. However, some children have challenging and demanding practices that are outside the standard for their age. In fact, behavioral disorders are the most common reason that parents seek the help of children's psychologists. In some cases, these behavioral problems are temporary problems due mainly to stressful situations, such as the birth of a brother, a divorce, or a death in the family. Other cases concern a model of hostile, aggressive, or incurred disruptive behavior

that is not suitable for the age of the child. The most common disruptive behavioral disorders include opposing challenger disorder (odd), behavioral disturbance (CD), and attention deficit disorder with hyperactivity (ADHD). These three behavioral disorders share some usual symptoms and can be exacerbated even more due to emotional problems and mood disorders. The psychology of children implies the search for all the possible roots of these behavioral problems, including brain disorders, genetics, diet, family dynamics, and stress, and therefore treat them accordingly.

4. Emotions: Emotional development involves studying what feelings and emotions are, knowing how and why they happen, recognizing their feelings and those of others, and developing effective ways of managing it. This complex process begins in childhood and continues in adulthood. The first emotions that can be recognized in children include joy, anger, sadness, and fear. Later, since the children begin to develop a sense of oneself, more complex

emotions, such as shyness, surprise, election, shame, shame, failure, pride, and empathy. Things that also cause emotional changes, as well as the strategies used to administer them. Learning to control emotions is more challenging for some children than for others. This may be due to their specific emotional temperament: some children simply feel more intensely and efficiently emotions; they are more reactive emotionally and find them more difficult to calm. Emotionally responsive children also tend to with enthusiasm and more relaxed than other children. It is the work of the psychologist's son, therefore, to identify the reasons why the child is having difficulty expressing or regulating his emotions and developing strategies to help him learn to accept feelings and understand the links between attitudes and behaviors.

5. Socialization: Strictly related to emotional development is social development, declared in a simple way, socialization implies the acquisition of values, knowledge, and skills that allow children to

relate to others effectively and contribute positively to family, school, and community. Although the stage begins shortly after birth and continues in adulthood, the age of early childhood is a crucial period for socialization. One of the first and most important relationships that the experience of children is with parents or the primary caregivers and the quality of this report has a significant effect on the following social development. In peer relations, children learn to start and maintain social interactions with other children, acquire conflict management skills, such as assuming, commitment, and negotiation. The game also involves mutual, sometimes complex coordination of objectives, actions, and understanding. Through these experiences, children develop friendships that offer additional sources of security and support to those provided by their parents. The factors that can contribute to an inability to develop the appropriate social skills of age include everything from the amount of love and affection; the child receives the socio-economic status of the family. Children who do not adequately socialize have difficulty creating and maintaining satisfying relationships with others, a limitation that many leads to adulthood. Areas A psychologist will try to face when working with such children include hostile or aggressive braking pulses and, on the other hand, learning itself in socially appropriate forms; Participate in socially constructive actions (such as helping, caring, and sharing with others) and develop a healthy sense of oneself.

## Psychology Tips to understand your child

Children's psychology is a vast topic. He informs him about the growth of an individual of the child until the end of adolescence and how every child is different from the other, not only physically, but also in his process of thought and personality. It is said that a child is like soft clay. Get shape to the way you die. Therefore, understanding that your child is crucial for all parents.

## Tips to Understand Child Psychology:

Knowing the psychological needs of a child is not easy, but it must be done. Children in different phases of development behave in different ways. A child from 5 to 6 years old behaves differently from a teenager. Realize and accept that you like, right, qualities (good or bad) is the key to be a good father. When you take them, as they are, they have a sense of security.

Here are some suggestions to help you understand your child:

1. Note that you need to satisfy your child if you want to understand it. You can simply do it because it's around you and looking at it. When you see it sound, asking for something, react in a certain way of situations, your interaction with others, etc., you can learn a lot about your general personality.

2. I know that your son's best friend, who does the son realizes that he is always there for him when he needs this, it can be his first step to achieve this goal. This

will make you feel safe, loved, and of course. Help him open up.

3. Spend the quality time with your child who is close to your son is not enough. Know it, better activities, like playing, cooking (children are always eager to help), clean the cabinets or their room, etc.

4. Praise Lady Child praises him for a good job done will have his self-esteem. However, overpressure can do it arrogantly and snobs.

5. Listen to your child; you will know it more. This will make you feel that you are interested in your life. This, in turn, helps strengthen the link between you two.

6. Talking about talking with your child: that interest can help you open. In this way, you can start conversations more easily and learn more about your child.

7. Give full attention while always talks about eye contact while talking with your child. In doing so, it will make sure that your child believes he is listening, and what he says is very important for you.

8. Give respect when the child talks about one of his insecurities, his fears, or any situation in which he became ashamed, does not laugh or ridicule. You have to understand it for a child (especially during your teenage years), it is not particularly easy to open. He must have taken a lot of courage on his part to do so.

9. Explain to children up to 5 to 6 will satisfy all the rules created by you or the decisions you have adopted for improvement. The real problem stands with adolescents. Blame your age. In such situations, I just try to explain why you had to make a particular decision or do something determined. At that time, you could be angry with you, but in the end, over time, you will understand.

10. Get the question of opinion for your opinion where it is necessary. Doing it will make it feel substantial and will increase your self-esteem.

11. Discover the reasons behind your behavior if your child was bad behavior, or showed an adverse reaction, try to discover the cause behind it. In this way, he will find where he was wrong as a father, and he will give him the opportunity to improve his adaptive skills.

12. Know your tastes and don't like knowing about what you want, and your son's dislikes will also help you understand them better.

13. Freedom of expression allows your child to express himself as he wants. You could take a look at how you think or what you want.

14. Do not be too curious for each parent is anxious to know what is happening in your child's life, especially in case your child is a teenager, but not being too

curious. Too much inquisitively on your part could make you feel that you do not believe in it, and this could end the link between you two.

15. Think about how important to think like them while talking or doing an activity together. This will give you a sense of familiarity.

16. Let your imagination take the wings while I go out with your baby, observe. I could see something very different from what you are viewing. Do not stop when you do it. This will help you get a vision of your inner world.

## Recognizing the issues with the Child's Psychological Development

A small child is sitting next to the window that looks like worried parents have an innate ability to understand when something is not right with their son. So how can you like a father a clear idea about what's going on? It is better to ask people who are close to their child.

## 1. Friends

ask friends who have children in the group of similar age and find out how their son is? They speak, they are able to write, eat alone, follow the instructions, etc. In the case of a teen child, you could ask your friends as he is at school, his behavior towards his peers and others, etc.

## 2. The Internet

Can also search for the Internet for your questions.

## 3. Teacher

during parent-teacher meetings, the teacher can also be able to shed light on the child's health and well-being. You can ask you if you've noticed something different in your child.

## 4. The donor of Care in Today's age

Many houses When Both Parents are working, you must take a babysitter / Ayah for your child. She is the one who must be with him anymore. Therefore, she is the best person to enquire when you feel something is wrong.

5. Pediatrician

A doctor can easily detect any deficiency in a child during planned visits for vaccination or check-up. 6. Psychologists will be the best person to answer any questions about the psychology of children. It can help in case of behavioral problems, such as depression, low self-esteem, anxiety/phobias, or different types of disorders, such as autism, ADHD, etc. In the kid.

# What are the distinct Psychological Disorders in Children?

Many psychiatric malfunctions in children are due to physiological, genetic constituent. However, there are many without physical causes. Some diseases can be diagnosed in advance in life, but some are not detected up to adulthood. Here is a list of them:

1. Deficit disorder with hyperactivity (ADHD) in ADHD, a child has problems paying attention and is hyperactive. Your actions are hard to control.

2. Intellectual disability, in this situation, the child

has limitations on mental functioning and is significantly influenced by adaptive behavior.

3. Autism spectrum disorder is a severe developmental disorder in which the child cannot communicate or interact. It affects the nervous system and the general development of the individual.

4. Perform the disorder is diagnosed during childhood or adolescence. Children with this disability have great difficulty following the rules and acting in a socially acceptable way.

5. Adjustment achievement: It is characterized by a group of symptoms, such as stress, feeling sad symptoms, or sparks without hope and physics to lose weight, etc. This usually occurs due to an emotional event seriously as the death of a neighbor, moving to some other place, change of school, etc.

6. Bipolar disorder: it can also be called manic depression or manic-depressive disease. It is

characterized by severe humor changes, hyperactive and socially unacceptable behavior, insomnia, depression, or an irritable state during a depressive episode, a feeling of being superior to other and suicidal trends in larger children.

7. Infant syndrome adopted: it is a disorder that is among some children adopted and occurs due to a series of psychological and emotional problems, such as linking with adoptive parents, an attachment to where they have previously lived or with people with whom they are often translated

8. Disorder of the stereotyped movement: it is a disease in which the person is involved in a repetitive movement not discovered that it could interfere with the usual daily functioning of the child. This disorder occurs mainly in children with autism, intellectual disabilities, or developmental disabilities.

9. Children's scaffolding: it is a rare disorder in children, but a severe mental disorder in which

children interpret reality in an unusual way. In this type of disturbance, the child can experience extremely disorderly hallucinations, disappointments, and thought and exhibited behavior that can affect everyday life.

10. Selective motility is a disorder of childhood anxiety and is mainly the inability of a child to talk and communicate in social environments such as school or any place where they do not feel safe and comfortable.

11. Slow cognitive time A care disorder in which the child seems to be in a different world and is sleepy, lethargic, hypoactive, and confused. It also moves slowly and is often found that it solves randomized objects for a prolonged period.

12. Disorder from the displeasure of gloomy mood is a mental disorder that occurs in children and adolescents. It is a case in which a child experiences extreme irritability, anger, and an outbreak of many intense temperaments.

# Parenting mindset

There are many keys to the success of the children, but often attention moves too much to the change of children as long as notice is stated on the essential beliefs that feed the decisions of parents. Without attending the thoughts and ideas contained in the mentality of parents, all long-term efforts will fail. Recently, I worked with parents who had a demanding dining room. It was a disaster. A true disaster. Why? Because I could not adjust your mentality enough to get out of fear and control and enter the world where your actions could teach. Then, understanding his perspective. His thinking about parenting is the first most vital step to deal with. It is like enrolling in the YMCA without changing your program or understanding how you can commit to a change of life. You don't want to take a Foster program, without first making you see if your approach keeps it a reality. For reality, I mean that your adoptive options are consistent with the way children learn. We will go to a brief overview of this. I really want you to recognize that each of these topics discussed below could consume an hour or two, but I offer this discussion to try to "start starting" your mentality so you can follow the guidelines provided on this site and start earning results. If you're fighting somehow, the most crucial step is to find a way of.

1. Renate the past: Let your frustration go about what happened in the past. Do not keep remembering your children about what happened last year at school. This undermines its success in innumerable ways. Let yourself go. Easier to say that? "Yes ... sure!" Critical for your success? "Absolutely!" When you throw the past, you free to face only at this moment. Not the other 324 times have had this topic. You do not have to bring all the most painful and frustrating moments. In fact, when you do it, you grew up right now. Actually, you are in a situation where you are emotionally looking for to administer dozens of emotional memories, and this can overwhelm you quickly.

When it is only this moment, free from the past, so it begins to respond to what is happening with a rational and reasoned approach. If the past continues to reach the present, you will always be overwhelmed by the most straightforward struggles. This is sometimes one of the most important problems to deal with. Many of us find it very hard to do so. We continue to see them trapped in "stories" in our head on our children. We can also start regret to our children and keep a wave of great anger. This is unhealthy. It will not allow you to find peace. It will not let you find a solution for parents. Because emotional reactions will always exceed the strategies, you are trying to implement. If you are in a place where you strive to be emotionally reactive, then you may want to consider parents' formation since this is an option to deal with the underlying thoughts and beliefs that cause this. Another option is to find a consultant in your area. A third option is to consider one of my products designed to help you release some of the thoughts and emotions that have yet passed. However, for now, it is essential to simply start to realize your history in the past. No matter how bad. That story can't help you and your child.

2. Focus exclusively on what you want: develop a clear vision of how you want your family to work and a clear sense of habits that promote success. Find out what you should do to build and encourage these habits. Concentrate on how it will be successful. It becomes clear about the principles and tries it over and over again. Remember: everything you approach will appear in your life. If you focus on the failures and deficiencies of your children, failures will increase. If you focus on your success, you will find ways to catch it. This immediately starts the process of putting your energy on what you want, instead of putting your energy on what you do not wish to (that is, the problems that happen). It also has a remarkable effect on your brain, preparing to start taking information and ideas that will make you more and more than you want.

3. Be patient: time is needed to feed successful habits. Establishing a new practice requires some time, both for you and for your child. Prepare for a learning curve from six to eight weeks. Sometimes a little less. And

sometimes a little more. During that period, he continues steadily and strikingly with the new principles he is implementing. How long does it take to cultivate a new lawn? It takes a few weeks, and you need an additional effort for those initial weeks. Right? It's the same here: you have to accept (only if you want the best things) that build new healthy models.

Is this true in every situation? NO!

You will find these products and some parent's suggestions that clearly indicate that you do not need 6-8 weeks to see the changes. This is true for specific situations in which it is possible to implement fantastic strategies for parents with unusual control over the environment.

# CHAPTER NINE

## Factors to encourage a mentality of growth in parenting

**1**. Always learning: short and simple, you can think of this sentence to remind you that it is healthy to be in the learning process; you don't have to know everything.

2. Connection, not perfection: This is my preferred growth mentality phrase to remember priority in my relationships is the connection; it is not perfecting all the details. It is useful to think when I point out of a family event that is not going as expected, when I want to support a friend and don't know the right words, or when I'm waiting for the right time to talk or play with my children. The connection, not bare perfection, more towards what matters.

3. They are in tune with my children, and I can make changes in our routines when necessary. Have you

ever felt like a failure when your routine is processed correctly, crumbling? It is useful to remember that your work is paying attention to this and making a change. 4. This was generally working for us (or I thought this would work for us), but I am authorized, I can make a change when things do not work. It can be challenging to have a growth mentality when something you thought would be perfect for your family. It is not. We put many stores in the breeding options of children, such as education, breastfeeding, food, feeding our children, childcare, sleeping arrangements, etc. It does not mean that the way to manage this decision is not necessary; I am. However, it is wrong to believe that there is a correct way and if you find it, everything will be fantastic. Sometimes, we have to make a change, and it can be humiliating and scary, but clinging to the models that do not work for your family is not a way to be a leader. What brings us to another prayer that helps you have a growth mentality in the upbringing of children.

5. Force and wisdom are required to recognize that the course must be modified, then take action to make that change.

6. I made a mistake, and I am a pretty big person to learn and move forward instead of clinging to something that doesn't work. Sometimes, it's nice to admit that we had wrong, but what was wrong when he stuck to something to something that doesn't work for you is not the answer. Aspiring him and go ahead, he is getting rid of.

7. It is never the wrong time to make a more favorable option. Sometimes I was captured to think that everything is a disaster, why worry? This sentence reminds me that making a more convenient option is always an option.

8. I can change direction. I can start again. A few days, we need one more—authorization of grants. You can start again.

9. I am an ongoing job, and this is part of that progress. It is good to have a vision of where you want to be, but sometimes it is easy to forget that the learning and growth process has excellent value. You are someone valuable at this time.

10. I always have the potential for growth. Yes, you do, you are not too old, too broken, too stupid. You have growth potential. It is useful for me to remember that I am not blocked to be a particular way; Through effort and time, I can change if I wish it.

11. What did I learn from this? Reflecting on what you have learned, even from the most uncomfortable situations, helps you grow.

12. The errors mean that I am learning. I always loved the song; my father sang me when I was a child who had a choir. He said: "Wow, you made a mistake, and you're beautiful for me." What sentence do you like to tell yourself to help you remember that you don't have to be perfect?

# Growth Parenting mindset

Did you know that you can teach your children a mentality that will help them become smarter? What happens if you told you that this same mentality could have a significant impact on how success and resistant your children are in adulthood. Would you like to know what is right? Welcome to the growth mentality of children! We will show you how to adopt a growth mentality that will help your children be more resistant to challenges. We will also share seven suggestions to teach your child to have a growth mentality so that he can help him expand his mental skills and become more student lovers. Started!

# What Is Growth Mindset?

Someone with a mentality of growth believes that their intelligence and skills can develop continuously during their lives. Basically, they think they can learn and, therefore, to be smarter and more qualified through the applied effort. Stanford Professor Carol Discitis, Ph.D., is the one that initially coined the term "growth mentality." Now it is commonly used in the circles of education and childhood development. After many years of study, Drive has discovered that there are some common points among children growing to be resistant adults, Adults that can effectively manage stress, and overcome challenges..

# CHAPTER TEN

## Growth Mindset Parenting: Tips for Success

1. Teach the children of your brain: the human brain is much more changing than we thought once. Teaching children who actually have the control that their brain grows through the actions they take is a significant improvement! Tell your children that your mind is like a muscle, most laborious work, determination, and practice they do, the more it grows. Children should understand that their intelligence is not on stone, can you change! Knowing that they can always learn new things if they are measured in an angular rock of the growth of the aging of the mentality. Once the children understand that the brain actually cultivates physical connections while practicing and learning new skills and concepts, they are excited about the learning process and live less of the errors.

2. Explain the different mentalities: Self-consciousness is an essential part of the growth of the equation of attitude. If you want children to use a growth-minded approach, it is necessary to help them understand what a fixed mentality is so they can recognize when they fall into one. All are a mixture of fixed growth and attitude. If we want to benefit from having a growth mentality, we must see when they operate for a fixed way of thinking.

3. Positive self-recreation: as the term "mentality" suggests, a lot of what is happening here is happening in your child's head. This is why it is essential to explain what your internal voice is and to talk to them like that voice sometimes wounds us. A large part of growth mentality growth is to teach children that if their words change, they can change their minds. This is a powerful lesson! (Also, for adults). If your child's notifications are frustrated, or you want to surrender, teach them how to exchange negative thoughts with more positive.

4. Praise the process: this can be called to recognize and encourage effort. He wants his children to understand that hard work and practice are what will help them achieve their true potential, not just talent. So instead of praising them when they win or get, they recognize the moments they fight and make efforts on what they are doing. I want your children to feel at ease with the fight. You don't want to be afraid to push you to reach the next level. Use phrases like: "I see that he worked hard to take it well ..." or "good work by taking such a difficult task." It will help your children continue to challenge themselves.

5. The power of Children grows and develops in different steps, which means that they will be continuously conducted on things that may not do it, perhaps their brother or equal. This can be super frustrating! You do not want your children in the "cannot" and renounce. What you want is that they realize that only because they cannot do something now, it does not mean they cannot do it in the future. And this, my friends, is still power. This small word is

a magical growth of the mentality of the children. It works in this way. Whenever your child says they cannot or remember them to add at the end of the sentence. It becomes entirely around and takes them out of a fixed mentality in a growth space.

6. Embracing: One of the best ways to model a growth mentality is to talk frankly by the mistakes you made, and what you have learned from them. This exposure to your children, who assumes risks and make mistakes are a natural part of the learning process. There is nothing like fighting through a problem, just to finally break it and solve it. Celebrate that feeling! At the end of the school day, ask your children what was confusing or what they worked very hard. After a failure, talk about what they would do next, next time. Frame it as an opportunity, not a yeast.

7. Let the labels drop: not to be continually saying your children who are "intelligent," "equipped," or "talented." This implies that they were born with unique skills and did not encourage efforts, practices,

or growth. Instead of motivating children, labels can put them in a box and communicate a fixed mentality. It is not what concerns the aging of the growth mentality. The development of a mindset of growth requires consistency over time. But once you put the base, perseverance, and problem-solving skills that your children develop can last a lifetime. Children will see errors as a learning opportunity, and they didn't stop smoking when things become difficult.

## How to strengthen your parenting mindset

A resistant father is not someone who shook his shoulders and simply brought suffering or difficulty with a thick, hard lip or low head. Instead, to be the resistant implies the reflection, the initiative, the courage to open up and learn in their emotions and experiences and learn about their best, is their support network. You are probably more resistant than you realize, and you have already overcome many stops, challenges, or errors on your life trip. This means that you already have strengths that you can draw. On the other hand, you can also resort to answers or lie that you no longer need it.

## Why mindset matters

Our mentality can significantly affect the degree in which we feel stress, as we respond to the importance and its impact on our experience of wellness and parenting. You can also influence how fast we can choose again after a demanding experience. This is particularly important for parents of children with complex needs since the challenges, results, and uncertainty are a frequent aspect. Stress has a physiological response. The more we work, the less able to get practical effects by solving skills or connecting with those interested. He sees his world of his "fear brain," who receives problems in the intensity of life or death and in black or black. This means that he will respond more impulsively and useless.

The first step towards strengthening his mentality involves considering his beliefs, experiences, and values and how they are "showing" in the way the father or response to his son. It means becoming aware of your automatic answers and asking if they are serving you. From here, you can explore different ways of thinking and respond to your parental experience.

**Here are eight minds of mentality to help you restrain unnecessary or induced responses to stress:**

1. Focus on the relationship. So much of the work of parenting a child with complex needs is the pressure to 'fix' and address behavior or deficits. This almost always comes more relaxed if you focus on your relationship first. Let go of struggling and battling for a moment, and just be with your child in the present, curious, open, and non-judgmental manner. Perhaps you can even look for a way to interact or have fun together.

2. Emphasize the imperfection. We often feel at ease,

and we love imperfect people because they give us permission to be ourselves. We appreciate the people who were wrong, laugh at themselves, and are open to their mistakes and limitations. This is also a great lesson to give our children, which can be loved and celebrated due to their uniqueness, peculiarities, and imperfections. The imperfect is, without a doubt, a much more refreshing and positive way to be. Check-in with what expectations or sizes use and let go.

3. Drill self-pity. It will be validated and kind enough for everything that is happening. Ask, what would be a kind and useful way to answer this? What would I say or act if this were my son or friend who feels like this?

4. Let the rope drop. You can often feel that you were in a perpetual war shot, with your children or yourself. Winning the "battle" is not always possible or worth it. Also, the irony to shoot for the firing of the war is that more shots, more energetic take out your opponent, and the problem becomes the problem.

This can be an image or metaphor useful to the point of complementation of point.

5. Notice when you fight and let the rope go. Go out for a while, even if you do not like what is thrown to the other side. This can often aid you to see more closely what is happening and free yourself to move forward.

6. Be curious and learn about your feelings and experiences. Make a pause and take some moments to be curious and open to what you feel, thinking, and experiencing. If this is too hard or abstract, start tuning your senses: warning what you can see, listen, smell, feel right now. This can create the distance you need to stop your stress or fear of the brain, feel safe, and be ready for your next "conscious" action. It is in this space where you can feel enabled to respond in the way you are more.

7. Pay attention to small things and pleasant experiences. Don't forget to be aware of the little

pleasures and moments of joy for your day. Take a picture, stop smelling a flower, feel the sun on your face, stretch your body in a way that gives you comfort, taste entirely a piece of fruit, or notice how you feel laughing during the game with your son. Often, these moments are resistant from our mind that solves the thought that we remain stuck in something that was not so good or potential problems in the future.

8. Learn how to fail or not learn. See errors or limits as an opportunity to learn and grow. Just because something has not gone well today, or there are still unresolved problems, this doesn't reflect who you are (or your son). The browsing aging of the collection is the curve, and continuous learning adjustment and failure is an essential component of this. No error, we cannot get the information we need to change or grow. The next time you fall to short, or something doesn't work with your child, try adding the word 'yet' or this time 'until the end of your self-assessment. Instead of "I am not good at ...", "I can't ...", or "I never ...", reform your comments to "I'm not good at ...", again

"or" I'm learning to ... "or" I didn't understand today, but maybe I maybe next time".

8. Recognize what has done well. This doesn't mean what you have donated correctly. Remember all the things you did and some little successes in your day. Be simply for you and your child about what is in progress, even if it may seem small for others or what is seen on social networks. If you get to your appointment, take your child to have breakfast, or perform 10 minutes of therapy together, it's a big problem for you and your child, then confirm this and the tenacity that beyond your own mentality works, don't forget to look for your support network and your ass team Ask for help if you need it.

# Tips for raising mentally healthy kids

Healthy mental children are prepared for the challenges of the world. I can deal with problems, bounce off failure, and deal with difficulties. Be clear; mental strength does not refer to action too difficult or deleted behavior. In addition, it is not a matter of being rude or reciting fading. Instead, healthy mental children are resistant and have the courage and confidence to achieve their maximum potential.

Helping children developing mental strength requires a three-point approach: teaching them to replace negative thoughts with more realistic dreams, helping them to learn their emotions so that their feelings do not control them and show them as actions, there are many foster strategies as follows:

1. Teach specific skills the discipline must be to teach your children to do better next time, not those who make them suffer for their mistakes. Use the consequences that teach specific skills, such as problem-solving skills, pulse control, and self-

discipline. These abilities will help the child learn to behave in a productive way, even in the face of temptation, difficult circumstances, and difficult stopping.

2. Let your child make mistakes to teach your child that mistakes are part of the learning process, so you don't feel embarrassed or ashamed to make mistakes. It allows natural consequences when you are sure to do it and talk about how to avoid repeating the same error next time.

3. Teach your kids how to build a firm self-speaking; it is difficult for children to feel powerfully influential when they bombard you with decodes or when they provide catastrophic results. He teaches his son to refrigerate the negative thoughts so he can think more realistic. Develop a realistic but optimistic perspective, can help children overcome difficult times and perform their best.

4. Encourage your child to face fears on the front of his son avoids something frightening; you will never get the confidence you need to manage to feel uncomfortable. If your child is afraid of darkness or is terrified to meet new people, help your child face his fear a small step at a time.

5. Allow your child to feel uncomfortable, even though it can be tempting to aid a child every time he is struggling, saving her from anguish will strengthen him that he is powerless. Forget the child, let me feel bored, and insist that he is responsible even when he doesn't want. With support and orientation, struggles can help the child build mental force.

6. Create characters Children need a strong moral compass to help them make healthy decisions. Work hard to instill your son's values. Create opportunities for life lessons that reinforce their values regularly. For example, underlines the importance of honesty and compassion, instead of winning at all costs. Children who understand their benefits are more

likely to make healthy decisions, even when others may not agree with their actions.

7. Great a priority gratitude is an excellent remedy for self-pity and other bad habits that can prevent your child from being mentally healthy. Help your child affirm all the good of the world, so even in their worst days, you will see that you have a lot of feeling grateful. Gratitude can increase the child's mood and encourage solving proactive problems.

8. Affirm the personal responsibility that the construction of mental force implies the acceptance of personal responsibility. Allow explanations, but do not excuse when your child commits an incorrect error or behavior. Correct your child if he tries to blame others as he thinks, he feels or behaves.

9. Teach the ability to adjust emotions to not calm the child when he is angry or encouraged every time he is sad. Instead, it teaches you how to deal with uncomfortable emotions, so you do not become

dependent on you to adjust your mood. Children who understand their feelings and know how to treat them are better ready to handle challenges.

10. The model of mental force roles showing your child how to be mentally healthy is the best way to encourage it to developmental force. Talk about your personal goals and teach your child, who is taking steps to become stronger. Make self-improvement and mental force a priority in your life and avoid things that mentally healthy parents don't.

# CONCLUSION

Parents play an essential role in the overall development of their children; It is the right guide for parents who develops the child's character. The aging is an endless job. It is not something you can get away from once the time comes, because children need their parents from time to time, to stay on the right path. Here is all you need to know about the role of parents in the development of your child. The advantages of good aging are that it increases children to follow the rules really well. While they are in situations where the rules know, they will feel very comfortable and safe. People who believe in being strict parents tend to be those who think that the provisions remain the same generations. What worked for their parents, works for them, and will work for their children.

Of course, there are consequences for a rigorous education that people don't like. Rigid parents bring children who are afraid to try new things or to break the rules. They live in constant emotional pain. They are confused with those who are if they feel even a little different from the person who applies the rules. If the rules do not apply, they don't know what to do, and they are baffled. As soon as the rules do not apply, they will be extremely uncomfortable. They tend to think that there is something wrong with them, something profoundly wrong, irrevocably. This could be really dangerous. It can lead to suicide as people feel they do not fit the world where they got up. Alternatively, children raised in a rigorous education often constitute a regulation of nothingness, and they will act as if that rule had been there all the time. The law could not make sense, or not be optimal, but it doesn't matter. What matters is that they know what to do, even if it's a non-optimal thing to do. It is more important to follow the practical rules for the people who believed in this way.

Is the world actually the same generation? If so, rigorous raising is a reasonable approach. If you already believe in strict paternity, there is no doubt that raising the chain is the way forward. You were created to take a life-based life approach, and there is no other alternative for you. However, if you think the world is changing and is changing rapidly, which increases children to be more flexible could be a better approach. If you believe that old rules may not be the best over time, you may want to grow children who think about what is happening and respond to situations as requested, given their objectives, instead of impressive goals on them and say that they always follow the rules.